More Praise for *Transformative Conversations*

"Despite the ideal of the 'academic community,' far too many of us live within the silos of our own programs or disciplines and long for a deeper connection with our colleagues to share our passions and heart and soul along with our intellect. *Transformative Conversations* is a book that is both visionary and intensely practical about how to create formation mentoring communities to break through the silos and create authentic community. This book is exceptionally timely as all of us face the stresses of budget constraints, dynamic change, and disruptive forces. Formation mentoring communities offer incredible hope drawn from the experiences of the four authors. Their stories and interludes are inspiring, and the book is a veritable toolkit for getting started. After reading an advance copy of the book, I intend to go out and form an FMC myself. The authors were challenged to write a book to start a movement, and this book just might do it."

—Ralph A. Wolff, president, Senior College Commission, Western Association of Schools and Colleges (WASC)

"This brief, beautiful, lucid book demonstrates how people meeting in small peer groups to explore themselves and what matters most to them can nourish, deepen, and transform themselves, each other, and eventually their larger community."

—Roger Walsh MD, Ph.D, University of California Medical School; author, *Essential Spirituality: The Seven Central Practices*

"This is a radical story about how to create a more intimate and relational culture inside the halls of higher education–which is no small accomplishment. This movement is occurring without a budget, a curriculum, or management approval. It is a great story of the power of intimacy and the small group as a positive revolutionary force. A must-read for those who long for higher education to return from the abyss of siloed isolation to its original charter as a cooperative learning institution committed to developing the whole person in service of the common good."

—Peter Block, author, *Flawless Consulting* and *Abundant Community*

"As a mediator who has assisted in settling dozens of cases involving institutions of higher learning, I only wish for the parties involved that this book had been available before differences devolved into wasteful lawsuits. This book provides practical guidance on how to create the space that can hold differences and transform the energy around them into creative rather than destructive forces, and it provides specific ways to avoid miscommunications that lead to needless conflict."

—Hon. Rebecca Westerfield (Ret.), JAMS: Judicial Arbitration and Mediation Services

"This book is filled with wisdom. While it addresses formation mentoring communities in academia, the lessons are applicable to any setting. The notion that 'hard to change' cultures, so resistant to expert intervention, are susceptible to transformation and renewal from within is heartening. The blueprint for transformation that this book provides is invaluable."

—Patrick O'Neill, president, Extraordinary Conversations Inc.

"In the 'superstorm' of writings about the crisis in higher education, this little gem of a book stands out like a mindfulness bell. It calls us back to the only thing that truly matters, the energy and wisdom buried in the minds and hearts of dedicated educators. Forget MOOCs and start organizing grassroots FMCs–countercultural, profoundly humanistic conversation groups. Watch deep truths emerge. After that, who knows what? Perhaps a twenty-first-century liberal education attuned to the coming generation's global imperatives: interdependence, sustainability, and mutual cooperation. Now there's a radical thought. Read this book please. It's all here."

—Diana Chapman Walsh, president emerita, Wellesley College; trustee emerita, Amherst College; member of the MIT Corporation.

Transformative Conversations

OTHER TITLES OF INTEREST

Alexander W. Astin, Helen S. Astin, and Jennifer A. Lindholm, *Cultivating the Spirit: How College Can Enhance Students' Inner Lives*

Jeanie Cockell and Joan MacArthur-Blair, *Appreciative Inquiry in Higher Education: A Transformative Force*

Laurent A. Daloz, *Mentor, Guiding the Journey of Adult Learners, Second Edition (with new Foreword, Preface, and Afterword)*

Sam M. Intrator and Megan Scribner, *Teaching with Fire: Poetry That Sustains the Courage to Teach*

Parker J. Palmer, *The Courage to Teach: Exploring the Inner Landscape of a Teacher's Life*

Parker J. Palmer and Arthur Zajonc, *The Heart of Higher Education: A Call to Renewal*

Sharon Daloz Parks, *Big Questions, Worthy Dreams: Mentoring Emerging Adults in Their Search for Meaning, Purpose, and Faith, Revised Tenth Anniversary Edition*

Daniel Wheeler, *Servant Leadership in Higher Education: Principles and Practices*

JB JOSSEY-BASS™
A Wiley Brand

Transformative Conversations

A Guide to Mentoring Communities Among Colleagues in Higher Education

∾ⓖ∽

Peter Felten • H-Dirksen L. Bauman
Aaron Kheriaty • Edward Taylor

Preface by
PARKER J. PALMER

Foreword and Afterword
RACHEL NAOMI REMEN & ANGELES ARRIEN

WILEY

Cover photo by ©Ken Canning/iStockphoto
Cover design by Michael Cook

Published by Jossey-Bass
A Wiley Imprint
One Montgomery Street, Suite 1200, San Francisco, CA 94104-4594—www.josseybass.com

Credits appear on p. 169

Jossey-Bass books and products are available through most bookstores. To contact Jossey-Bass
directly call our Customer Care Department within the U.S. at 800-956-7739, outside the U.S. at
317-572-3986, or fax 317-572-4002.

Wiley publishes in a variety of print and electronic formats and by print-on-demand. Some
material included with standard print versions of this book may not be included in e-books or in
print-on-demand. If this book refers to media such as a CD or DVD that is not included in the
version you purchased, you may download this material at http://booksupport.wiley.com. For
more information about Wiley products, visit www.wiley.com.

Library of Congress Cataloging-in-Publication Data
Library of Congress Cataloging-in-Publication Data had been applied for and is on file with the
Library of Congress.
ISBN 978-1-118-28827-6 (paper); 978-1-118-41986-1 (ebk); 978-1-118-42129-1 (ebk);
978-1-118-49624-4 (ebk)

Printed in the United States of America
FIRST EDITION
PB Printing 10 9 8 7 6 5 4 3 2 1

CONTENTS

Contents

PREFACE

Margaret Mead famously said, "Never doubt that a small group of thoughtful, committed citizens can change the world. Indeed, it is the only thing that ever has." Clearly, Mead overstated her point. Some social change has come from small groups of cunning, malevolent people whose commitments have ranged across the continuum of evil.

Still, Mead's point stands. Every movement for positive social change that I know anything about has been initiated by groups of the sort she describes. Of course, successful movements find ways to rally more and more people around their flag, consolidating and deploying collective forms of "people power" to make an impact on institutions and societies. But even as movements for social change expand, the effective ones continue to depend on small group "base communities," not merely to make decisions about strategies and tactics but to sustain the energy and morale of their adherents in the midst of arduous struggles.

Transformative Conversations: A Guide to Mentoring Communities Among Colleagues in Higher Education focuses on the development of small groups called formation mentoring communities (FMCs) on college and university campuses. FMCs differ from professional meetings of the kind that normally fill our days. An FMC would not be a planning meeting, a task force, or a problem-solving session. Nor would it be a gathering to develop a joint professional project. The group's "project," so to speak, would be the group's members themselves. The agenda would consist of reflecting on our work and life, remembering our callings, exploring meaning and purpose, clarifying personal values, and realigning our lives with them. The goal of an FMC would be to use meaningful conversations to reinvigorate ourselves, our work, and, by extension, the academy.

Anyone who knows even a little bit about academic culture knows that gatherings such as this are, to say the least, countercultural. So it is important to know that the authors of this book are four accomplished educators who serve in four very different academic settings. They not only believe that it is possible for faculty and staff to gather for these personal and professional purposes; they know it is possible because they have convened and hosted such groups on their own campuses. Their book draws on lessons learned as they experimented with bringing colleagues together and discovered both the potentials and the limits of their on-the-ground efforts to create FMCs.

It is common knowledge that universities are highly resistant to transformation. As the old saw has it, "Changing a university is like moving a cemetery. You don't get much help from the inhabitants." But FMCs have the potential to create transformational energies, as they help faculty and staff reclaim the values that brought them into the profession in the first place and help them find ways to bring those values to life amid the increasingly challenging conditions of twenty-first-century academic life.

I am convinced that the greatest threat to the highest values of any of our professions is the institution in which that profession is practiced. Attorneys who go into the law because they want to serve the cause of justice must constantly resist the deformations of the justice system. Physicians who go into medicine because they want to help people achieve wholeness, even those who are terminally ill, must resist the deformations of the health care system. And teachers who go into the public schools or professors who go into the university to help educate young people must resist the deformations of educational institutions.

Because the threat to professional values comes not from without but from within, transformation must come from within as well. The institutions that house our professions are too complex and opaque for outsiders to know where the levers for change can be found. Insiders alone have the necessary knowledge and access. But insiders who have been co-opted by the self-protective and self-serving logic of institutions—or who have simply given up in the face of all those discouragements—will never be agents of institutional change. The energy and thoughtfulness for transformation will come only from insiders who have reclaimed the commitments that brought them into their profession in the first place and have found the courage that comes from saying, "I'm not going to let anything or anyone rob me of my core values."

Formation mentoring communities have great potential for laying the groundwork for institutional transformation by helping educators help each other engage in self-examination, discuss challenging circumstances, and remember and explore personal values, meaning, purpose, and calling. I hope this book will be read and put into practice by enough academics that the green shoots of change will begin to spring up in places where its principles and practices are embraced and embodied.

Parker J. Palmer
Madison, Wisconsin
November 2012
Founder and senior partner, Center for Courage and Renewal
Author of *Healing the Heart of Democracy*, *The Courage to Teach*,
A Hidden Wholeness, and *Let Your Life Speak*

FOREWORD:
REMEMBERING
WHAT THE ANCIENTS KNEW

What catalyzes deep change for human beings is always an appeal to the heart. The heart is the seat of our courage to remember and live by what matters most profoundly. It has been at the center of all sustainable personal transformation and at the foundation of all social movements throughout time.

Sometimes a simple invitation is an unexpected appeal to the heart. It was through such an invitation that this book, *Transformative Conversations: A Guide to Mentoring Communities Among Colleagues in Higher Education*, began. Four years ago, we both said yes to an invitation from the Fetzer Institute to join a group of peers and explore the concept of intergenerational mentoring in the hopes of learning what this approach might contribute to revitalizing the innate values of higher education. Originally we joined this process as senior mentors, along with others of our generation known to us—people whose company we enjoyed over the years and whose scholarship we respected. Collectively we all shared the hope of passing on what had been learned in the course of a lifetime of teaching to others who were younger.

What we encountered was something far different: an experience of intense personal and professional learning and growth in the company of four young men who themselves were learning and growing. Through this project, we two women in our seventies, who had known each other for thirty years, met four brilliant, gifted, and competent men in their thirties and forties and entered into a mutual relationship that was new to us. Despite our years of mentoring experience, we were completely unprepared for the initiatory process that would be galvanized for all six of us or how profoundly we would reshape, stretch, and amplify each other individually and collectively.

Over the three years of the project, all six of us became more than we were at the beginning. We discovered we each had within ourselves certain core values that were like seeds dropped into soil: when exposed to acceptance, honesty, trust, and genuine friendship, they could sprout and blossom into change in ourselves and in our work.

Over time each of us was mentored by all the others, sometimes formally but often in quiet moments over a meal or a cup of tea. We seniors both became convinced that we were learning as much from the four young men as they were learning from us. As with most of our senior colleagues in higher education, we two who had known each other for decades and had long admired and supported each other's work had never mentored one another before. Indeed, most academics of our age and stage have not been mentored by anyone for many years.

Gradually, over time, we became a true formation mentoring community. The six of us catalyzed and called forth new aspects and dimensions from each other, and at different times and in different ways, we discovered in the relationship between us the heart of higher education. Within our relationships to one another, whether working, writing, or in weekly phone conversations, we experienced the grace and ease of a steady, nonconceptual wisdom that existed within and among us that was subtle, palatable, and contagious. This innate wisdom allowed us to explore together what the poet Gerard Manley Hopkins called "the dearest freshness deep down things." We discovered that those deep-down wisdom things are profoundly valuable, transformative, replicable, and inextinguishable. We all experienced the ability to develop fresh capacities and grow. We brought out the best in one another, and we continue to do so.

What we collectively experienced and discovered is a dimension of human nature that indigenous people everywhere embrace and honor: the power of community to evoke and nurture the perennial wisdom that resides in each of us and simply awaits our engagement. All genuine learning involves a radical remembering of this timeless providence of who we already are and what our intrinsic nature intends to bring to life through us. Within this hidden and unifying continuity of perennial wisdom, we are brought back again and again to ourselves and each other, to our deeper remembering of our humanity and its highest ideals.

Remembering ourselves and our original values is not something that we can do alone. Much in today's world separates us from our core values and makes it difficult for us to remember ourselves. We need others to befriend the hidden wholeness within us, to see it even before we can, to believe in it and reflect it back to us so that we can recognize it as our own. Relationship allows us to find our way home together, to reown our hopes, our promise, and our calling. For most of the world's oldest cultures, mentoring in the perennial wisdom is a natural lifelong process both personally and professionally. Intergenerational community supports it by initiatory rites, apprenticeships, meaningful conversations, and guidance from individuals of all ages. In traditional cultures, wisdom is not age bound. It is considered a mutual learning process that occurs naturally between all people. It is through learning from those both older and younger than ourselves and reflecting our deepest values back to one another that we begin to live up to our full human potential. What we experienced in the three-year journey the six of us took together was the immediate relevance of this ancient approach to the challenges of higher education and the modern world.

This experience has been so profound that it seemed important to share it with others. Ultimately it was the four young men who became the torch-bearers to ignite the transformative flame of formation mentoring communities on their respective campuses. This is their book, "a deep-down thing" that is accessible to everyone and can evoke the wisdom within us all. What is inextinguishable in the human spirit is connected to the heart, the place of self-remembering that allows us each to commit ourselves; to care enough to act; to contribute, create, and serve the greater whole; to learn to become better human beings; and to pass our wisdom on to future generations. This commitment is at the core of all meaningful and relevant education.

We are grateful to have participated in the process by which this book came into being and to have met the four remarkable, courageous men who now offer it as a gift to all educators and academics. Those who feel the need to grow and live closer to their authentic values on a daily basis can take this book and create a place of refuge and self remembering, a place to befriend the dream of a better world in themselves and in all others.

Angeles Arrien
Rachel Naomi Remen

Transformative
Conversations

INTRODUCTION

In the interest of full disclosure, perhaps we should begin by saying that we are an unlikely group of authors. We are all midcareer academics who under ordinary circumstances would have found little in common to talk about—and indeed would never have even met. But in early 2009, each of us received a written invitation to become part of an experimental project on intergenerational mentoring communities sponsored by the Fetzer Institute. From the start, this felt unfamiliar yet important. The list of senior mentors and visiting elders read like a who's who in their respective and diverse fields.[1] The thought of working with such distinguished and insightful leaders in higher education was enticing and humbling, but we were also intrigued by the questions at the heart of the project: *Could the mission of the academy expand beyond the development of intellect to the cultivation of the whole human being? Is it possible to create a "new university" with an expanded focus to better prepare students to respond to the unmet needs of today's world?*

Accepting this invitation meant making a three-year commitment to participate in seven retreats in various parts of the country and work together to create and implement a yet-to-be-determined project. This was not a commitment to be taken lightly. There were many good reasons to politely refuse this opportunity. All of us were busy, focused on our careers, and facing the challenges of balancing work, family, and additional projects to which we

1

had already overcommitted ourselves. In addition, we all lived in different parts of the country, adding to the logistical challenge of working together. Yet we all found that we could not easily dismiss the questions posed in the invitation. These questions followed us as we went about our lives and nagged us in the spaces between our obligations. Whatever our individual reasons, eventually we all said yes to the invitation.

Twelve other midcareer academics from varied backgrounds and diverse academic disciplines accepted the invitation as well. At our first retreat meeting at the Fetzer Insitute in Kalamazoo, Michigan, we were asked to self-select into groups of four junior faculty and two senior mentors around one of four areas that would define the scope of our three years of work: Leadership, Pedagogy, Ethics, and Formation. After a rather lengthy and uncomfortable period of indecision, the four of us eventually found ourselves in the least coveted corner of the room: the one under the banner of "Formation."

This was not a moment of instant recognition and colleague-ship. It was more evident what we did not have in common than what we did. Our university contexts, roles, and disciplines did not immediately unite us in common conversation. Two of us are from large research universities and two from smaller liberal arts colleges, and we hail from psychiatry, education, history, and cultural studies. More specifically:

- Dirksen Bauman is chair and professor of American Sign Language and Deaf Studies and coordinator for the Office of Bilingual Teaching and Learning at Gallaudet University.
- Peter Felten is assistant provost for teaching and learning, director of the Center for Engaged Learning, executive director of the Center for the Advancement of Teaching and Learning, and associate professor of history at Elon University.

- Aaron Kheriaty is the director of residency training and medical education in the Department of Psychiatry at the University of California (UC), Irvine.
- Ed Taylor is a professor of education and vice provost and dean of undergraduate academic affairs at the University of Washington.

We were very fortunate to be joined by Angeles Arrien and Rachel Naomi Remen as our two senior mentors. It was evident that their wisdom, rich experiences, and varied backgrounds would greatly add to the group:

- Angeles Arrien is a cultural anthropologist, author, educator, and president of the Foundation for Cross-Cultural Education and Research who lectures and conducts workshops worldwide.
- Rachel Naomi Remen is a physician, author, and medical educator who is a clinical professor at the University of California, San Francisco, School of Medicine. She is a pioneer of relationship-centered care and relationship-centered medical education, and her formation course for medical students is taught in more than half of America's medical schools and seven countries abroad.

At the beginning it wasn't clear how we would fit and work together, we had all connected with the idea of formation in higher education, so we tentatively began to explore what formation meant to each of us. We wondered if a concept like formation, which is at home in disciplines far outside of academia, could find a place in our educational institutions. We wondered if formation could become a dimension of our relationship to our students and what it might mean for academics to attend to each student as a whole person (formation) rather than just a person of intellect (education). We also began to reflect on how we as faculty were changed (formed or de-formed) by the various institutional pressures of higher education. We began to wonder what formation would look like for us. Eventually we saw that we were as much in need of formation as anyone else. And that was the beginning.

Through e-mails and weekly phone calls, we began to reflect on the conditions that foster growth (formation) and envision a specific sort of conversation designed to generate these conditions. Could such a conversation in small communities become an incubator for the growth of all who participate? Could this growth be some form of mentoring, a concept familiar to academics yet usually seen in a more limited way? We began to expand our ideas of mentoring and envision a mentoring beyond professional competency—a mentoring of the whole person. We looked at existing models of mentoring and thought about what mentoring might look like in a group context. Gradually our concept of mentoring expanded past the usual understanding and practice of mentoring the youngest among us, students and junior faculty, to include the entire academy, from the most senior to the most junior and all administrators and staff.

We ultimately envisioned small intergenerational groups or minicommunities where the fundamental orientation of each member would be to support the aspirations of every other member, where we would help each other uncover, strengthen, and manifest our deepest values in all our relationships, including those with our colleagues as well as with our students. Where we would engage in an ongoing conversation with a small group of colleagues about our desires for a richer life and more fulfilling work and find the support and encouragement to move toward transforming those desires into daily practice.

We imagined that such community conversations could reinvigorate the academy in the pursuit of its aspirations and foundational values and eventually transform higher education itself. If these groups were to take root on college and university campuses, we envisioned an academy in which faculty and staff were mindful that they were doing more than preparing students for professions: they were engaging the whole people in a process of perpetual growth and formation. We envisioned an academy in which faculty and staff were challenged to communicate honestly with each other and with students, thereby modeling habits of relationships and respect that students could carry into their personal and professional lives.

We were emboldened in this somewhat quixotic endeavor by the fact that such large-scale change has already been ignited through the work of our mentors in the fields of medicine (Rachel Naomi Remen's *Finding Meaning in Medicine Groups*) and in personal transformation (Angeles Arrien's *Four Fold Way*).[2] We saw the potential of these groups as something exciting and positive, an opportunity for renewal. Such opportunities for support, transformation, and growth were not widely available within our four institutions of higher education. In fact, they were not available at all.

We came to call these small groups formation mentoring communities (FMCs) and began to think through how these groups would differ from the other professional meetings, groups, or committees that fill our days. An FMC would not be another committee or a therapeutic group. It would not be a planning meeting, a gripe session, or a time in which members address a campus problem and "get things done" or develop a joint professional project. The group's "projects," so to speak, would be the people themselves. The agenda, if there was an agenda, would consist of reflecting on our work and life, remembering our calling, exploring meaning and purpose, clarifying personal values, and realigning our lives toward them. Ultimately the agenda was to reinvigorate our work through conversation and, by extension, reinvigorate the academy itself.

We thought about ways to promote these ideas and encourage people to convene these kinds of conversation groups. But we realized that before we could ask others to do this, we each needed to pilot a group on our own campuses and learn what worked and what did not.

While our mentors, Angeles and Rachel, had extensive group process experience, the four of us did not fully know what we were getting into or what to expect. We all had years of university teaching experience and had mentored scores of students, but none of us had organized or facilitated quite this sort of egalitarian conversation before. And while each of us had reflected on questions of meaning and purpose in our work, sometimes talking with colleagues or friends about these things, none of us had pursued these conversations with much depth or commitment. But in the end, we found that our relative inexperience made us open to being surprised and turned out to be one of our strengths.

Our mentors drew on their experience with groups and suggested that FMCs needed certain guidelines to create the sense of personal and professional safety that would enable the kind of exchanges we envisioned. We determined that the groups should be small, not more than six people, and meet regularly. Each member of the group should be on equal footing regardless of academic rank or role. Group members should share facilitation, and careful attention should be paid to establishing a hospitable space of safety, honesty, and trust.

All four of our campus groups operated with these same key guidelines, yet the actual shape, size, and structure of our FMCs were quite different so as to best fit the group members and institutional context:

- At UC Irvine, Aaron's group consists of five physicians in the School of Medicine, most of whom belong to the Department of Psychiatry and all of whom teach medical students and residents. Over time, a few of the members left the group when they departed from the institution, and others have taken their place.
- At Gallaudet, Dirksen's group began with just two other colleagues, both of them his former students within the master's program in Deaf Studies who have continued to teach and do research at Gallaudet. Experiencing that three people were not a large enough group, they eventually added a fourth member.
- At the University of Washington, Ed's group began with members of the UW staff, a faculty member, and a graduate student. After continued discussion about the concept of formation, mentoring, and friendship, Ed expanded his FMC presence on campus by coteaching a freshman seminar on personal transformation using texts that invited students to form communities while planning their own journeys.
- At Elon University, Peter's group of five has been constant from the start. The four faculty and one student life staff member are different in many ways, but all had been in their roles on campus for about five years when the group began.

Despite our lack of expertise, the significant differences between our academic cultures, and the composition of our groups, these community conversations have all been transformative. On all four campuses, members have expressed sincere gratitude for the opportunity to participate and have shared how these conversations have led to meaningful changes in their professional, and sometimes personal, lives. Some have commented that it has rekindled their passion for teaching and helped them to recollect and reinvigorate what drew them to this work in the first place. Others have spoken of how the experience has changed their perceptions of others in the university and how they have found the courage to speak up in challenging circumstances. They have also shared how their group experience has had a significant impact on their teaching and academic relationships outside the group setting, initiating a ripple effect across the campus community.

Like the other members of our groups, we have found it a privilege and an inspiration to participate in these FMCs. This work has helped each of us to grow and discover who travels with us beneath the masks we all habitually wear on campus. At each of our universities, our FMC group has evolved from an experiment to a rich source of meaning and community in our work and lives. We have also witnessed how the transformative nature of our conversations has moved beyond our small circle of colleagues. While it would be delusional to think that our institutions have been fundamentally transformed as a result of these small, guerrilla-like meetings, it would also be a disservice to underestimate the potential for wider change. We have each, in our own way, witnessed instances of personal and wider institutional transformation and how they have shown up in the classroom, in the department, and throughout the university. We discuss some of these ripple effects and the potential for wider, institutional transformation in the final chapter of this book.

Our participation in these groups has reminded us how infrequently those of us in higher education—faculty, staff, and administrators—are encouraged to stop and reflect on our work and our lives. The opportunity for reflection generally takes place once a year during an annual evaluation. But these reviews are most often perfunctory and do not encourage reflection in depth. Over the past few years, we have found that FMCs provide a radically different evaluation system of our teaching, scholarship, and service. Instead of being ranked on a point system by our colleagues and administrators, we are called into a more profound process of reflection on enduring questions: Who am I as a teacher, as a scholar, and as a colleague in service to the institution? As testimony to the transformative nature of our conversations, we have all developed a profoundly different notion of service. As opposed to the common perception of service as a dreaded committee assignment, we have, in our own ways, come to see that our teaching, our scholarship, and all of the other work we do is in service to the future of our society and our humanity. Having the opportunity to remind each other of the higher aspirations and significance of our work has been downright invigorating.

The success of our groups, despite the wide diversity of our academic settings, suggests that this model can take hold on your campus as well. And what is remarkable is that this all comes from a simple concept and process. FMCs are oriented first toward helping participants attain the most essential goods proper to higher education: knowledge, wisdom, character, and citizenship, for example. It is therefore a place of cooperation rather than competition, a place of trust rather than suspicion. The goods it fosters are not scarce resources, for knowledge and wisdom do not diminish when they are shared. Members of an FMC do not engage in a zero-sum game, where one person's gain is another person's loss. The common academic viruses of envy and rivalry do not find traction in an FMC; indeed, FMCs are a sort of antidote to these viruses. To put it in Aristotelian terms, an FMC is a context in which authentic collegial friendships can grow—relationships where a person is not treated as a means to other ends but as an end in himself or herself.

Transformative Conversations invites you to do what we have done, but in your own way. It offers a window into our experience, what we've learned and how we have grown along the way as conveners and members of these groups, and it serves as a practical guide to convening and sustaining FMCs. Our experiences and reflections are captured in the "From Our FMCs" text boxes throughout the book.

We believe that you'll find ideas and approaches in this book that will work for you on your campus. We have been in your place of wondering if convening an FMC is worth the time and the effort. We can answer that with a resounding yes, and we offer you this book in a spirit of colleagueship, possibility, and adventure. We hope it will enable you and those in your FMC to hear with new ears and see with new eyes the calling that first drew you into academia. We also hope it strengthens and deepens your best aspirations and sustains and invigorates you in your work and life.

Finding the Time and Space for a More Meaningful Professional Life

The alarm rings and the ritual begins: coffee must be made; kids must be fed, dressed, and shepherded to school with homework, lunches, and signed field trip forms; dogs must be walked, cats fed, books and papers collected. We launch ourselves out the door of our home life, which will be there waiting for us when we return.

Then we make the sherpa-like trek to campus, bearing bags, books, papers, computer, and coffee in hand. After negotiating the parking, we wend our way to the office, wake the computer from its sleep, and the e-mail triage begins: "Where is the draft of the book chapter that was supposed to be done last month?" "Can I change groups?" a student wants to know, "because so and so won't cooperate on this and that." And then "the note taker," bless her heart, has sent the minutes from the curriculum committee that must be reviewed before distributing, and the meeting is tomorrow.

And then the rest of the day unfolds: the meeting for the faculty governance committee, a fifty-minute class with twenty-five students, office hours with students already lined up outside the door, and then we skim the assigned reading for the next class that begins in fifteen minutes. And the hour that was carved out as space for writing and scholarship is overridden by a departmental meeting since there was no other time to meet.

Then, time to eat, check more e-mail, and the waning time left to ride the day roughshod into the evening, where the home life awaits with all its demanding ties—dinner, homework (the kids' and our own), housework—and then we collapse in a heap of sleep.

And then: the alarm rings and the ritual begins again.

Within the thicket of the days, when is there time to hear even an echo of the calling that brought you into the academy, the calling that took you by the shoulders and looked you in the eyes so deeply you could not look away? And even more difficult, when is there time to remember the original calling of higher education in the first place? When is there time to reflect on the relation of our work with students to its impact on society and humanity? When do we have a chance to view our students as citizens of the world and our teaching as a reflection of ourselves and our highest aspirations for our students as they enter the world as young adults? When is there ever a chime, like the calendar reminders that pop up on our computer screen fifteen minutes before a meeting, for us to summon up the aspirations that we had for ourselves, our students, our university, our nation, our world? When is there time to be reminded of the initial spark that ignited the flame? When is there time to stop, look, and listen?

CHAPTER 1

What Is a Formation Mentoring Community?

Formation mentoring communities (FMCs) are opportunities for a small group of colleagues to explore their individual hopes, aspirations, and purposes and to reflect on their common problems, challenges, or concerns. An FMC is a time and place to be in conversation with others who are holding our deepest well-being at heart, who have no vested interest other than contributing to the best that we all can be. It is a place of safety where we find acceptance and are listened to generously, where we don't have to fight for space or limited resources. This makes these groups different from our typical ways of working and talking together in higher education.

While FMCs initially may feel like unfamiliar terrain, we have found that they are not an alien landscape to many of us. The ecology of these groups—formation, mentoring, and community—has deep roots in higher education. In this chapter, we explain how our conversations and readings led us to understand the potential and promise of FMCs.

~◦～ *From Our FMCs:*

Reimagining the University

I would like to see a revolution where we recreate our university as a humane place that truly lives up to its mission statement to be "an academic community that transforms mind, body, and spirit and encourages freedom of thought and liberty of conscience." This always seems more possible to me after one of our formation mentoring community conversations than … after a faculty meeting.

Formation

Since our group began our conversation by sitting under a sign reading "Formation," we initially spent a lot of time wrestling with that concept. For some of us, *formation* invoked a rich and honorable lineage of human learning and development, while others were wary of some of those same traditions, wondering if formation must necessarily lead to a particular intellectual or spiritual outcome. Because the word *formation* is often absent from higher education today, we reached back to read and discuss texts, many of which claimed not only that formation is a component of education but that all education is formation.

Over time we came to understand formation as a process that involves the integral development of the whole person: intellectual, emotional, professional, moral, and spiritual. Formative education focuses on supporting people in developing their shared human capacities, sometimes framed as strengths and virtues, as well as cultivating each person's particular gifts and talents. This contrasts with the deformative processes that may occur in higher education, bending us away from our aspirations or limiting our capacities by confusing criticism with learning, specialization with progress, and practicality with purpose.

The formation process includes cultivating a sense of meaning in one's work. For some it may include discerning and responding to a life calling or vocation. Formation requires an honest search and open desire for greater self-knowledge and so is premised on a commitment to engage in self-examination. It involves not only an awareness of one's personal strengths or talents but also a humble recognition of areas of weakness and vulnerability. The process of formation promotes good habits of mind and heart, ways of seeing clearly and acting well. Formation is the work of a lifetime; our formation is never finished. However, formation may not always be an intentional process about which we are fully and consciously aware. Our identities and characters are forming all the time through our experiences, our decisions, and our actions.

~ⓐ~

We often forget the grandeur of the world we inhabit as well as the mystery of our lives. The simple act of stopping to reflect, and then of holding our awareness—gently but firmly—on these forgotten dimensions of the world and our lives is a service and even a duty.

Arthur Zajonc, Meditation as Contemplative Inquiry

In the wisdom traditions that guided our conversations, we noticed that formational work often builds on threshold experiences. In mythology, this sometimes is represented by being at the water's edge or coming to a gate. Do you cross into the unfamiliar or step back into what is known? Crossing the threshold involves the conscious awareness of a liminal moment or event, a significant juncture that may call for change, transition, reassessment, or conversion. These experiences typically cause individuals to face fear and even failure; however, they also can become times of previously unrecognized resilience, strength, or virtue. They can be times of growth, even transformation.

One goal of FMCs is to help us recognize these threshold moments and support us in acting with purpose when we stand on the brink and as we go about our daily work.

Mentoring

The most common approach to mentoring in higher education assumes that the mentor possesses some knowledge that can be communicated, modeled, or in some other way passed on to the protégé. In graduate programs and across the academy, students are often mentored into a "craft" or "trade" (to use these terms very broadly) by faculty advisors. Conventional mentoring programs for staff and faculty, where they exist at all, typically involve pairing a junior person with a senior colleague. The latter instructs the former on the ins and outs of the institution and the field, giving practical advice on career advancement. Such mentoring is important. You want your orthopedic surgeon to have been trained by the best teachers; you want the historian who wrote the book you're reading to be skilled in her craft. Mentoring as apprenticeship is necessary in education and professional life.

Formation mentoring goes beyond these more focused and end-oriented practices. It is not merely imparting information or helpful advice; it is not imposing ready-made solutions from the outside on complex professional or personal situations. Formation mentoring comes from a deeper notion of mentoring. To borrow a metaphor from Socrates, for whom all learning is but remembering, the mentor is like a midwife. The mentor gives birth to knowledge by drawing out what was already implicit within the one being mentored. In the course of this kind of Socratic inquiry, answers and solutions may emerge that the person had not previously seen. This kind of mentoring has as much to do with listening, with what might be called conversational hospitality, as with talking and instruction.

～☯～

Mentoring is as much (or more) about asking the right kinds of questions as it is about giving sage advice. A good mentor poses "questions that go straight to the heart and the heart of the matter. . . The mentor knows that each life has a distinctive contribution to make to our common life, and if this contribution is not made, a life is diminished and the commons is impoverished.

Sharon Parks, Big Questions, Worthy Dreams

Sharon Parks, a leader in the field and practice of mentoring, has described the five essential gifts of mentoring as recognition (being seen and heard), support, challenge, inspiration, and accountability. We never outgrow our need for this constellation of gifts within our personal and professional lives, and FMCs provide a context in which we as professionals within higher education can offer these gifts to each other.

Thus, another important and distinctive feature of FMCs, which contrasts with more typical mentoring arrangements, is that the entire group (the mentoring community) and each of the group's constituent members mentor one another. While one or two people may have initiated the FMC and some members might be more experienced than others, no one within the group is designated as mentor or protégé. Rather, mentoring within an FMC is relational: each person is a mentor to the others, and each

17

person is being mentored by the others. This requires a community of trust and honesty, something that is not always present in more hierarchical mentoring relationships.

Community

Formation mentoring flourishes in, indeed requires, a particular kind of community—one aimed toward formation and nurtured by a certain kind of conversation. Work in higher education can often be isolating (writing, reading, grading, researching, prep, and more prep) and exhausting (participating in committees, task forces, councils, and more committees). All of this is important and necessary for maintaining the integrity of our disciplines and institutions. But it can also be draining, fraught with tension as people jockey for position and power, and tiring as people spend inordinate time on seemingly trivial topics. Isolation, or being together only in tense or exasperating ways, is a significant barrier to meaningful relationships and communities on campuses.

To counter this common experience, we recognized the need to cultivate deliberately different relationships and communities— ones that nurture rather than deplete. This is precisely the central aim of FMCs: to create a new and different sort of space among colleagues. The FMC's purpose is to contribute to the ongoing formation of the individual and the community in higher education.

For the four of us, our campus FMC groups have become that: places to renew and recharge, to remind ourselves why we do our work and what we aspire to in our lives. Formation mentoring communities enable us to find moments to come together and connect. Formation mentoring rises in this space and then flows out to fill the many cracks in the rest of our professional and personal lives. The foundation of a deeper relationship created through these periodic conversations creates a wellspring of support.

Relationships are the hinge on which FMCs turn. The collegial friendships that develop in these small communities, characterized by solidarity, concern, reciprocity, and mutual respect, provide the context for the work of formation. So in an important sense, the formation of these genuine communities is as important as the individual formation that takes place within them. An FMC provides on a small scale a space, a commons, where members are no longer "bowling alone" (to borrow Robert Putnam's memorable phrase).[1]

                              ✺

Each citizen should play his part in the community according to his individual gifts.

Plato

We recognize that we may sound hopelessly old-fashioned by conscripting words like *formation, mentoring,* and *community.* To be sure, there has been a degradation of our language, such that these once-noble concepts have been hollowed out. Even the words *academy* and *academia* have suffered corrosive influences: "that's merely academic" is a dismissive way of indicating that the thing in question is divorced from everyday reality or from the concerns of reasonable people. The word rarely evokes, as it once did, one of civilization's most noble and foundational enterprises.

Rather than making an academic (there's that word again) argument in favor of recovering what is good and noble in all of these terms, we propose that the practice of participation in an FMC may be what is needed to counter the stresses and the cynicism that are prevalent in higher education. Among other things, perhaps the quiet and persevering work of FMCs—communities where participants use sustained conversation to assist one another in pursuing a life of purpose and meaning—can help to revitalize not only our language in higher education but also the rich and worthy aspirations that such words were meant to convey.

One of the surprising outcomes of our FMC experience is the gentle but persistent reminder that there is more to life, more to our careers, than the minutiae of daily work. Through participating in the FMCs and engaging in these mentoring conversations, we are better able to see the connections between the hourly tasks and the larger direction of our work. This in turn can remind us to hold both ourselves and our institutions accountable, not just to a personnel committee or an accrediting body, but to our larger mission of transforming our students and shaping our world. While such a large task of social transformation may be so daunting that individual effort seems pointless, those of us in education are used to working on the scale of one student at a time. There is no reason, though, to forget the formation of ourselves and our colleagues along the way, one individual at a time.

Contrasting FMCs with Other Groups

One way to gain an appreciation for the unique nature of FMCs is to contrast them with other groups. FMCs are markedly different from the typical committees that are familiar to all in higher education. A committee has institutional mandates and goals, specific tasks to complete, a clearly delineated agenda, and a leader who chairs the meeting. Committee members often jostle for position and advocate for their own interests. In a committee, each of us is expected to always bring our competence and expertise, rarely our questions or doubts, and never our struggles or vulnerabilities. Committees play important roles in higher education, but few academics want yet another committee on their list of weekly or monthly obligations. Committees typically take from participants and give back little in return. An FMC, by contrast, is a cooperative, egalitarian arrangement that focuses on the good of group members themselves rather than on external outcomes or achievements.

FMCs also differ from therapeutic groups. The members of an FMC offer one another forms of support, and in this way, the group may be indirectly therapeutic in the broad sense of the word. But group therapy is designed to focus on participants' emotional wounds and disorders; it aims to directly assess and heal such wounds. An FMC, by contrast, exists to help participants explore, form, articulate, and live out their values. By taking an interest in each other, asking open and nonjudgmental questions, and listening attentively, FMC members encourage one another to grow professionally and personally. In an FMC, the focus is on strengths and virtues rather than wounds and weaknesses. Vulnerabilities are acknowledged and accepted, but the group's purpose is to encourage our capacities, explore our hopes and aspirations, and inspire our work.

The Lineage of FMCs

Our concepts and practices of FMCs developed gradually over the course of our three years together. We were influenced along the way by the work of others who have made important contributions to the theory and practice of dialogue, mentoring, and formation in higher education. When the six of us convened for the first time as part of a larger gathering of educators, we had recently read Parker J. Palmer and Arthur Zajonc's *The Heart of Higher Education*. Our initial discussions about integrative education were

21

encouraged by their call to a more holistic approach to our work, and more attention to "first and last things."[2] To reach beyond the practical and mundane, Palmer and Zajonc reminded us, we must rethink the very foundations of learning and knowledge and the very purposes of higher education.

As we probed the relationship between formation and education, we recognized that the concept of educating the whole person found a ready home in intuitions inspired, for example, by the work of Ignatius of Loyola. But could a concept like formation of the whole person, in contrast to education focused solely on the intellect, find a home in diverse institutions and settings? Many philosophers and educators, from Plato and Socrates through the contemporary advocates for educating global citizens and ethical leaders, have maintained that it can and must. Along these lines, we discussed early in our project whether universal values could or must ground this work of formation. Among other sources, we considered the work of scholars in the positive psychology movement (e.g., Martin Seligman and Christopher Peterson) who make the case for universal human character strengths and virtues that are conducive to happiness and human flourishing.[3] We also discussed Alasdair MacIntyre's claim in his book, *After Virtue*, that the development of these virtues occurs not so much as an individualistic project of self-improvement, but rather in the context of communities characterized by shared practices, ends, and aspirations—communities like those that exist (or should exist) in our institutions of higher education.[4]

Our focus on community and formation contrasts with most of the literature on mentoring in higher education. Lois J. Zachary's influential books, for example, offer a coaching model of mentoring that, while moving away from traditionally hierarchical practices, still presume a two person mentor-mentee relationship.[5] Other books on this topic typically frame the relationship as "mentor-mentee," as Bland does, or define it as Johnson does in his practical 2007 guide: "Good mentoring relationships (mentorships) in academic settings are dynamic, reciprocal, personal relationships in which a more experienced faculty mentor acts as a guide, role model, teacher, and sponsor of a less experienced . . . protégé."[6] That is a perfectly valid approach to mentoring in higher education, but it is not ours.

As we convened our FMCs and explored models of mentoring, we were also fortunate to have the personal and intellectual influence of Sharon Daloz Parks, who, along with Arthur Zajonc and Mark Nepo, served as a mentor for the larger project convened by the Fetzer Institute. Parks's essential book, *Big Questions, Worthy Dreams*, encourages mentors to go beyond a narrow, operationalized process of instruction and be daring enough to explore and cultivate the deeper aspirations and hopes of the person being mentored.[7] She argued that questions about meaning, purpose, and faith indeed have a place in mentoring and in the work of higher education. She has persuasively argued that as valuable as one-to-one mentoring-protégé relationships can be, the strength of transformative learning that is now needed may require mentoring communities or mentoring environments.

Early on we also read David Bohm's *On Dialogue*, which influenced our understanding of the group process and dynamics of FMCs.[8] Bohm distinguishes dialogue, which has creative and unifying effects, from mere discussion, which tends toward analysis and competition. Typical discussions, according to Bohm, are characterized by a sterile process "batting the ideas back and forth" in an effort to score points and win at a sort of intellectual table tennis game. Dialogue, by contrast, is a cooperative enterprise that facilitates mutual exploration and truth seeking. Bohm's definition of dialogue inspired our thinking about the nature of conversations within FMCs, as did Peter Block's *Community*, Sara Lawrence-Lightfoot's *Respect*, and Craig Neal and Patricia Neal's *The Art of Convening*.[9]

As we proceeded into the second and third years of our project, we gradually came to appreciate another important intellectual influence on our work, Aristotle's understanding of friendship (see Books VIII and IX of his *Nichomachean Ethics*). We did not originally set out with the intention of cultivating friendships, either among ourselves or in our FMCs on campus. While we spoke early on of providing space for "collegial" relationships, we did not frame our invitations to participate in FMCs as an occasion to develop friendships. But as we reflected on our experiences with our project, we found our conversations came more and more back to the language of friendship.

All of us were quite comfortable on campus with the imperfect forms of friendship that Aristotle describes: professional relationships that come and go, based primarily on utility or convenience.[10] We have plenty of professional colleagues and acquaintances with whom we can make pleasant conversation at the faculty meeting or partner for a period of time on a joint project. But through our FMCs, we found opportunities for the development of deeper and more lasting friendships—more meaningful relationships where each colleague is now valued as an end in himself or herself. This was, we recalled, precisely what Aristotle characterized as real friendship, and it has become an important outcome of our experiences with FMCs.

Finally, it would be impossible for us, the four authors, to overestimate the influence of our two mentors, Angeles Arrien and Rachel Naomi Remen, on our work with FMCs. Both of these extraordinary women have pioneered work on formation and mentoring in the context of the communities they have founded.

Rachel's Finding Meaning in Medicine groups and Angeles's Four-Fold Way wilderness retreats have affected thousands of participants from around the globe. Their life work has been rooted in wisdom traditions that speak to profoundly human values and aspirations. Angeles and Rachel have been our Socratic midwives, giving birth to our work with FMCs, our writing process, and our collective conversations. Indeed, they have shown to us not just mentorship but friendship.

When we began our work with FMCs, Rachel suggested that our task was to "start a movement"—a notion that we thought was impossibly grandiose until we recalled that she and Angeles had already done just that, transforming medical education and individual lives in this country and beyond. Because of the work they have done, because of who they are, these two women made the incredible sound credible. They gave us courage to do work that we never would have attempted without them.

With their gentle presence and firm commitment, Angeles and Rachel have accompanied us along every step of this journey. Formation mentoring communities not only stand in the lineage of their prior work; they are yet another extension of their work. Angeles's and Rachel's fingerprints are found on every page of this book, and *Transformative Conversations* is as much theirs as it is ours.

Message in a Bottle

Perhaps you have found a measure of what we consider success in higher education. You may be regarded as an outstanding teacher, achieved tenure, or garnered some degree of recognition for your work; colleagues may consider you to have made important contributions to your field. But in our experience with peers in the academy, a certain discontent, a vague feeling of dislocation, is found not only among those who are denied tenure or who have not yet been published. It is equally (if not more) distributed among the so-called successful. Those who stand at the top of the tenure ladder may look around and wonder, *Is this as good as it gets? Is this all there is? Is this really why I earned a doctoral degree and joined the academy?* Perhaps beneath the surface of our successes, our accomplishments, our accolades, there remains a dim memory of something else—an inchoate sense of longing for something more.

In his essay "The Message in the Bottle," the late novelist Walker Percy described our predicament in this way.[1] He compared us to a castaway on an island who had lost his memories in a shipwreck. The castaway soon discovers that the island happens to be a pleasant and fully inhabited place. It has "a remarkable culture with highly developed social institutions, a good university, first-class science, a flourishing industry, and art."

This is a place perhaps not too different from the modern academy. The castaway has no apparent reason to feel alone, for the local islanders receive him warmly and he integrates fully into the community. And yet try as he might, the castaway never feels fully at home. The problem is not with the island, or the people there, or even its institutions, but with the fact that he is a castaway—a wayfarer and a pilgrim. That is his predicament, and he cannot be cured by the island's resources. So he looks to the sea, waiting for something that might speak to his predicament.

The castaway, in his loneliness, often takes walks along the beach, looking out over the sea. From time to time, he comes upon bottles washed on the shore. Each one contains a slip of paper with a sentence written on it. Some bottles contain what he considers "knowledge," and others contain what he calls "news." Bits of knowledge are just that: bare facts, scientific findings that are true but have no direct bearing on his situation (e.g., "Lead melts at 330 degrees"). But bits of news are *news for him* precisely because they speak to his predicament as a castaway (e.g., "There is fresh water in the next cove").

Our castaway in academia is no different: he has a sense that all is not as he would have hoped, and he is bombarded with messages; most are knowledge, few are news. His response to another piece of knowledge is to simply confirm it, reject it, or, most likely, just add it to the many messages piling up in his inbox: "You have been invited to participate in an ad hoc committee on performance improvement according to the latest accreditation standards." Knowledge, not news.

But then he receives the following; "I invite you to participate in a community of respect, regard, acceptance, and trust, in which others want to see and encourage the best in you." This indeed is a piece of news from across the seas. This is a bottle with a message precisely for him.

Let us suppose this castaway accepts the invitation to join a formation mentoring community (FMC). He may discover that "the island" of the university turns out to be populated by other castaways, many more than he could have imagined. The loneliness, one of the core features of his predicament, has already to some extent been relieved, for he is not, as he previously thought, the only one who is looking for something more. There are fellow travelers, wayfarers, pilgrims with whom he can find company, and even friendship. There are other castaways who understand his predicament and can remind him of things he has perhaps forgotten.

There is now a space on the island—a space within the academy—truly different from the others that he had previously inhabited. This community is not a lifeboat that takes him off the island; he may in fact never leave the island. But he can live there feeling less like a lonely exile or a solitary alien. In fact, his contribution to the island culture is enhanced by what he gains from his participation in this community. How do these "castaways" begin to connect with one another in an FMC? In the service of mutual mentoring, FMC conversations often involve personal storytelling. By telling a meaningful story, a person who has entered the group out of a sense of isolation (e.g., "I'm the only person who has had this experience or feels this way") often is able to leave feeling less alone. When we realize that our individual and unique stories—our supposedly isolated and unrepeatable experiences—resonate with others in the group, something surprising happens. Percy writes about this in relation to reading literature, but it holds also for the experience of telling or hearing stories in the context of an FMC: "That which seems most individual about oneself, the quirky unspoken part of one's experience, even the unspeakable, is suddenly illumined as part of the universal human experience. The exciting paradox of [storytelling] is that it is in one's own unique individuality that one is most human."[2]

So that peculiarly meaningful experience about which we nevertheless had doubts, which puzzled or confused us and caused us to wonder, "Am I crazy for thinking this way? Will anyone have a clue what I'm trying to express?" may turn out to be the very thing that most lights up another member of the group. "Yes! That's how it is! I didn't know anyone had ever felt that way!"[3] Through such connections, the members of an FMC can become a sort of community of castaways.

CHAPTER 2

Cultivating Growth

Conversation in Community

Our two-year experience at all four of our campuses attests to the power of a small community of peers to encourage and support individual creativity, authenticity, integrity, and change. Personal growth requires encounters with the new and the unfamiliar. But it can be difficult to take steps into the unknown. The nonjudgmental camaraderie of a group of colleagues who are also growing allows risks to be taken in ways that are measured and supported and often makes possible the sort of growth that could not occur in isolation.

Despite the significant differences within our FMCs, all the faculty and staff who participated were able to identify and reconnect to their core values, revitalize their individual dreams, and renew their commitment to goals that serve as the foundation of their work and their lives. Our experience suggests that the nature and quality of the relationships formed within these small communities create an environment where participants are able to reflect on and embrace these kinds of changes. FMC relationships feel different from those more commonly experienced in the day-to-day culture of our individual campuses. Within each FMC, we deliberately and collectively create new ways of relating to colleagues and to ourselves. The sorts

31

of interactions we develop, experience, and practice within an FMC can become habitual and extend to relationships far beyond those within the community itself, eventually creating a groundswell of change in the interactional culture on campus.

We have incorporated many of these qualities into the interactional agreements, practices, and guidelines for creating FMCs (see chapter 3). We offer the following reflections on them as background and encouragement as you contemplate creating your own FMC. You can also use them as brief readings for your groups—starting points and reflection questions to deepen and enrich conversation in your FMC:

Hospitality
Safety
Courage
Honesty
Trust
Diversity
Humility
Accountability
Friendship

Hospitality

Hospitality: An open door, a welcoming gesture, a warm greeting. Come in, be at home, relax. You will be cared for, you will be heard, you will be seen. Hospitality comes from the word *to host*, to create an environment of welcome. What precedes hospitality is typically the acceptance of an invitation, which brings us into a new experience. Accepting this invitation, crossing the threshold, and joining the group involve decision points. Often our choice to continue with a new group is determined by our initial experience of how we are being hosted. Genuine hospitality goes a long way toward quieting the internal monologue of self-consciousness, clearing space in which we can reveal ourselves in conversation and allowing our idiosyncrasies and failings to have a place at the table with our successes. When we feel welcomed into a new space, we are more likely to bring our full selves, without apologies, with fewer worries about fitting in. Being in a space where we know that we are listened to invites us to be ourselves and bring forward the person we are striving to become. In short, hospitality is a condition for growth.

We rarely talk about hospitality within the academy. A world defined more and more by a scarcity of resources discourages an ethic of generosity and ceases to see the value of space or time for anything that is not deemed practical. In a time of diminishing resources, colleges and universities have become less hospitable environments. Often there are fewer staff to work with an increasing number of students. There also is a growing dependence on part-time, adjunct faculty, and thus intense competition for the few coveted tenure track positions and decreasing research funding, especially in the humanities. Having to constantly hustle, maneuver, or compete in challenging environments can leave individuals wounded and diminished.

Our work within FMCs has helped us see that we do not need food, drink, or a budget to generate hospitable environments. These groups can cultivate an intentional space and time for each of us to be who we are and talk about the person we want to become. Once we are accustomed to creating a hospitable space regularly in the context of an FMC, we see that it does not require more than we already possess. With these regular experiences, we are more likely to open hospitable spaces within our office hours and in our classrooms. "The classroom where truth is central," Parker J. Palmer writes, "will be a place where every stranger and every strange utterance is met with welcome."[1] Every reader of this book, every member of the academy, carries the potential for hospitality within him or her: generous listening and a simple act of letting others know they have been seen, heard, and appreciated. This kind of generosity consists not so much in giving as in understanding.

As we become more accustomed to creating such spaces, we learn, as Palmer recognizes, that there are paradoxes at the heart of hospitable environments: they must both be open and yet have strong boundaries; they must be safe but not too safe; they must be charged enough with an edge that real growth can occur. "Hospitality," Palmer writes, "means receiving each other, our struggles, our newborn ideas, with openness and care."[2]

⌒⊛⌒

When someone deeply listens to you
it is like holding out a dented cup
you've had since childhood
and watching it fill up with
cold, fresh water.
When it balances on top of the brim,
you are understood.
When it overflows and touches your skin,
you are loved.
When someone deeply listens to you
the room where you stay
starts a new life
and the place where you wrote
your first poem
begins to glow in your mind's eye.
It is as if gold has been discovered!
When someone deeply listens to you
your bare feet are on the earth
and a beloved land that seemed distant
is now at home within you.

John Fox, "When Someone Deeply Listens to You"

For Reflection and Conversation

1. Describe an experience when someone listened deeply to you.
2. What makes you listen with attention to someone else?
3. Reflect on the nature of hospitality within your department or unit. Are the expressions of hospitality genuine and sustained or performative and perfunctory?
4. Hospitality usually implies a host and guest relationship. Yet in an FMC, we are all hosts and guests. How can we create a communal hospitality?
5. Making learning environments more hospitable does not necessarily mean that we wait on our "guests" and they don't have to lift a finger. How can we convey to students that they can make themselves at home in this space of learning—that if they want something, they can help themselves, but be sure to get enough to share with others and that they too have a role in helping to create and sustain the hospitality of the space?

Safety

When people talk about safety, they typically are thinking about attending to basic needs, being cautious and secure: wear a helmet; wait for the signal to cross the road; stay behind that solid wall. Unfortunately, there are reasons to seek such safety and be cautious in academia. Even on campuses that are collegial and supportive, the culture of higher education is typically characterized by judgment, criticism, and evaluation. The way to be safe is to avoid any possibility of perceived failure, often by walling oneself off from others. The result of such a risk-averse culture is the lack of opportunities for growth, transformation, and surprise. Yet as Parker J. Palmer reminds us in *The Courage to Teach*, within truly hospitable and safe environments, we are more likely to go out on a limb, to let go of the reins of self-consciousness that bind us to the known.[3] Knowing that we are ultimately held within the embrace of safety, we can fall down, make fools of ourselves, and put our shortcomings on full display, and yet still be encouraged, appreciated, and respected. In this sense, safety is a critical condition for growth and transformation.

Formation mentoring communities are incubators of such safe environments because there is no assumption that members must be perfect. Unlike the annual evaluation that documents and quantifies any perceived failures (not securing a journal to publish an article, for example, or negative teaching evaluations), an FMC encourages discussions of personal and professional risks, so by reflecting on our "failures," we can be transformed by them for the better. Although FMCs cannot completely eliminate the culture of judgment that often characterizes the academy, by creating a space that is hospitable, participants can work together to develop and nurture the confidence that they are safe within the group. Knowing that we are safe from professional or personal harm opens up possibilities for personal transformation. As the group evolves, the meaning and significance of safety changes and expands. After a meeting or two, for example, members feel confident that asking a seemingly simple question or raising a specific concern will spark a fruitful conversation. They might raise an issue and request a particular kind of response from the group, such as, "I'm trying to understand different perspectives on this," or, "I'm stuck in the details and need help thinking about the big picture of that."

Over time, group members feel safer to go more deeply into questions closer to the core of their work and their identity. When we feel safe, we don't talk only about how to perfect a research technique or how to respond to the revise-and-resubmit comments on a manuscript. We don't ask only how to manage a difficult person on a committee or how to write a better exam question for a course. When the environment is perceived to be safe, we are able to ask questions that touch on our more significant challenges, fears, and hopes such as, "What should I do after I earn tenure?" "If I say yes to this enticing opportunity, what might I have to say no to later?" "How can I better align my work with my values?" "How can I more effectively balance my professional and personal life?"

This kind of safety is not only growth enhancing for individuals; it also becomes part of the mortar that holds the FMC together. All the mental and emotional energy that previously went toward keeping up our defenses and maintaining appearances can now be placed in the service of honesty and creativity, of thinking more about others rather than about ourselves. This frees us to listen more attentively, to be more present and available to the other members of the community. Together we can experience the freedom to explore our identities, the courage to take risks, and the willingness to be caught learning.

Safety Allows Us to Take Risks

Safety is important if we are to take real risks within an FMC. A trapeze artist without a safety net is foolhardy. With the net, however, she can safely try things on the trapeze that she would not otherwise attempt, knowing that if she falls, she will be caught. A shared sense of safety within a group functions like a safety net, allowing group members to venture beyond what is comfortable and familiar and knowing that the group will catch them if they fall.

For Conversation and Reflection

1. Describe a risk you were willing to take because you were conscious of a sense of a safety net. Did this risk lead to new discoveries?

2. What are some conditions you would identify as important for creating a safe space for conversation and dialogue? What agreements do you need to make to others, and others need to make to you, in order to sustain a safe conversation?

3. How can safety be established, sustained, and renewed as a condition for growth within specific contexts, such as department meetings, classrooms, and personal relationships?

4. Make a note of times when you do not feel safe, either within or outside the academy. How does this feeling affect your behavior?

5. Think about the many people you come into contact with during your days. Do you sense that they feel safe in your presence?

Courage

Courage is a basic condition for growth, yet academics don't talk much about it. Perhaps the courage we exhibit every day is too nuanced to be easily recognized or even noticed. A firefighter is courageous when he charges into danger and saves a trapped person. In comparison, what is courageous in the life of an academic? Yet many situations in higher education require courage. Certainly standing up in front of three hundred students or peers to give a lecture requires courage. Telling a student that he will not pass your class, disciplining a student for behavior in a dorm, telling a colleague her merit review was less than stellar: these could well be described as moments requiring courage. And a certain amount of courage is required in cutting budgets during challenging times.

But academic culture often encourages us to keep our heads, and especially our hearts, down, working toward extrinsic rewards like promotion and tenure. Few of us, however, went into higher education with the primary goal of earning tenure or being granted an endowed chair. Instead, we were imbued with a passion for learning and discovery, for understanding the world a little better and perhaps for even making it a more just place. But over time, it is easy to lose this passion, to play it safe and settle for the more tangible, yet perhaps less fulfilling, marks of success.

One of the fundamental purposes of an FMC is to evoke and strengthen the courage to recognize and act on our core values. An FMC enables us to reconnect with those passions and align our work more closely with them. FMCs tend to focus on process more than outcomes, so the essential questions are not how to do something but why to do it. In the setting of our customary busyness and pressure for results, just taking the time to ask, "Why?" can be an act of courage. Making the time to act on that "why" even in small ways has the potential to have an impact on the larger academic community. It may lead others to be brave enough to connect with their passions and ask the larger questions too. Understood this way, starting or joining an FMC can be considered a courageous act.

The kind of courage we discovered in our FMCs is tied closely to the etymology of the word *courage*, from the Middle English *corage*, "the heart as a source of feelings, spirit, confidence," and from the Latin *cor*, "heart." In this regard, courage is not so much about single acts, decisions, or behaviors as it is a virtue that emanates from the heart and can be cultivated over time.

This kind of courage also sustains and deepens an FMC. In a highly competitive and judgmental culture, investment in relationships requires courage. Many of us are accustomed to relatively superficial ways of interacting with colleagues. The greeting, "How are you?" is often not heartfelt or even meaningful. The response is often the same. But in an FMC, this simple question reflects deep caring and is backed by a commitment to listen generously. Both the question and the response pose risk and vulnerability. The speaker may admit to a lack of knowledge or competency, and the listener might concede just as much uncertainty. Their shared commitment to speak truth becomes the driving force for needed change. To engage in this small act is a step toward a daily practice of courage.

The courage that is cultivated within the group often begins to affect our daily lives outside the FMC. We may become empowered to speak up in department meetings and ask the deeper, larger questions. We may shift from talking about our values to acting on them. Courage, it turns out, has a trajectory—from within me, to between us, and then into the larger world. As the sculptor Constantin Brancusi writes, "To see far is one thing: going there is another."[4] As we journey on our professional and personal paths, FMCs support us to take the courageous steps needed to go further.

~◎~

Whatever course you decide upon, there is always someone to tell you that you are wrong. There are always difficulties arising which tempt you to believe that your critics are right. To map out a course of action and follow it to an end requires—courage.

Ralph Waldo Emerson

For Conversation and Reflection

1. Describe a time when you or someone else you know acted courageously. What specifically made this an example of courage? What conditions allowed this to happen? What risks were taken?

2. Identify an issue you are struggling with that requires you to act with courage. What is preventing you from acting courageously, and what support do you need to embolden you to step forward?

3. What kind of courage is required of those who work in colleges and universities? What is the role of courage in your scholarship, teaching, and service?

4. What are the conditions necessary for individuals and groups to walk in this world courageously?

5. What stands in the way of courageous acts as part of your day-to-day life?

Honesty

Honesty seems like a straightforward condition for growth. Just tell the truth. To everyone. Always. If we do that, we'll all be better off. Simple enough?

Honestly, no. No matter what Shakespeare wrote or what we remind elementary school children, honesty is not only not the best policy; it is not a policy at all. Honesty is an orientation toward ourselves and others; it shapes how we speak and what we choose to talk about. The capacity to think and speak honestly nurtures growth. Honesty enables a clear-eyed vision of what is and what could be. Yet some of academia's harshest and most diminishing behavior comes under the guise of honesty: the anonymous reviewer who zings the writer, the conference presenter who gets publicly dressed down during the question-and-answer session, or the use of disrespectful and humiliating critique in a faculty meeting. Yet does honesty need to operate in this way? And is such brutality really honesty at all? Is honesty truly synonymous with judgment, or is it something quite different and distinct? Certainly there is an honesty that uncovers, affirms, and promotes what is good and true in all things. An honesty that is a fundamental prerequisite to growth.

An FMC is based on the commitment to honestly speak about ourselves, revealing our inner worlds, meanings, aspirations, hopes, inadequacies, fears, and doubts. When such honesty toward oneself is expressed within a group, an opening is created—an invitation for each of us to reflect on our deeper truths that we might

41

otherwise mask even from ourselves. Such revelation in the context of safety is a critical condition for growth and transformation. Without these conditions, it is nearly impossible to share what is most meaningful, to step beyond previous limitations and grow. To be able to hold ourselves in all of our imperfections and failings, and to do so in the witness of others, engenders a sense of self-compassion and compassion within the group. We are seen not only through the lens of our outwardly promoted successes but through our deep humanity—equally loved, equally acknowledged, and equally instructive. Such complexity allows us to be faithful to who we are and to be more fully present for others.

FMCs are honest and safe, supportive and encouraging of change, allowing each member to be both vulnerable and strong—in other words, to be whole. It is important to remember that the conditions that foster honesty and safety include respect, openness, curiosity, creative engagement, and trust. When these qualities are consistently present, honest communication emerges. Ultimately honesty is the heart's expression of what can best support and empower the inherent goodness in another human being. Essentially honesty is the embodied alignment of mind, heart, word, and action. It is considered an aspect of truth telling with compassion rather than blame or judgment.

In order for the honesty muscle to be exercised, the participants of the group have to show up for the workout. This is where the team may be greater than the individual player. Through open sharing and respectful listening, the group as a whole can coax greater and deeper expressions of honesty. The group's overall ecology of honesty enables an individual to see the story she should tell in the first place. In this sense, our selves are formed within the FMC, where honesty is the magnetic north.

~∞~ *From Our FMCs*

What Does Honesty Look Like in an FMC?

I think honesty comes from each of us bringing our incomplete thoughts and imperfect selves into the group. That's not a typical posture for many academics. We are trained to know, to analyze, to dissect. We are trained to say "yes, but ... " Knowledge and critique may well be important aspects of honesty, but they are not all that is necessary. Honesty requires some vulnerability too. Honesty requires you to stand for something rather than to pose as the critic of all. Honesty requires putting things together, not just tearing things apart. Still, that's not to say that all of our conversations are equally honest. Sometimes we put our own distraction or politeness in the center of the table. Honesty in a community is partly about presence. Honesty is partly about imperfection.

~∞~

I want to unfold.
I don't want to stay folded anywhere,
because where I am folded, I am a lie.
And I want my grasp of things
true before you. I want to describe myself
like a painting that I looked at
closely for a long time,
like a saying that I finally understood,
like a pitcher I use every day,
like the face of my mother,
like a ship
that took me safely
through the wildest storm of all.

Rainer Marie Rilke, "I Am Too Alone in the World, and Not Alone Enough"

For Conversation and Reflection

1. Imagine yourself unfolding as Rilke suggests. What truths would emerge?
2. There are many adages worldwide that state that the truth will set you free. What prevents you from opening to a deeper truth in your life, with your family, in your health, in your work?
3. When do you feel encouraged to be honest—or discouraged from being so?
4. What is your reaction when you have been a witness to others' revelation of personal truths?
5. Reflect on the nature of honesty within your teaching, scholarship, and service.

Trust

Being welcomed into a hospitable space is a great gift. It allows us to be seen and heard for who we are. But for many of us, this may be unfamiliar territory and a bit unnerving. It may be one thing when we're seen as the smarter-than-thou self who stands behind a podium in conferences and classroom lectures but another thing when we're revealing the searching, imperfect, curious self, exploring why we didn't feel more confident in the face of a particularly intelligent and challenging student or an intimidating department chair. Yet when we speak from a definitive, all-knowing position, there is no curiosity for new knowledge and insights. Without some degree of risk and vulnerability, there can be no growth. Growth can occur only when we step out into unknown terrain, cross that threshold, unsure of where the journey will lead, unsure of the ground our feet are on.

Habitually, we test uncertain ground before fully leaning into it. We put out feelers to see if we trust where we are going enough to take the next step. Trust allows us to go further, taking greater risks, becoming more vulnerable, and risking more of ourselves. In this way, trust is a condition for transformative growth. Trusting those with whom we are in conversation allows our self-editor—the internal censor that rethinks and revises what we say to fit an imagined sense of what should be said—to take a break. All the mental and emotional energy that goes toward keeping up our defenses, maintaining appearances, and so on can be placed in the service of honesty and creativity and the pursuit of a robust collection of opinions and ideas. Trust allows a more authentic exploration of a real self, a real voice, a real sense of individuality. It opens up opportunities to explore questions we didn't even know we had.

If we trust others, we may speak honestly without fear of what they will think, without worries that they will someday "use this against me." When we feel safe among the others, then our emotional life, not just our intellectual life, is welcome. We can speak of our hopes or aspirations, our struggles or difficulties. There is no need to keep up a pretense that we have it all together, that the stress never gets to us, or that we're keeping it all "under control."

Trust also frees us to listen more attentively, to be more present and available to the other members of the community. The default mode of competition in the academy can give way and allow mutual cooperation, mutual cultivation of our individual and collective growth.

Finally, we have found that having trust in others just feels good. It feels good to be held and lean into others and know we will be supported. An FMC is not a typical academic department meeting or group, and that is a good thing. Since trust is so foundational to these communities, it is worth taking the time for the group to revisit this issue and ensure the process is being respected.

Another layer of trust is necessary in FMCs. For the group to thrive, you need to trust the process. It's unlikely that you'll have a firm agenda each time your community gathers together. The conversation may stick close to an agreed-on topic, or not. The group needs to develop ways to talk about the process itself so that everyone can continue to trust that despite the twists and turns along the way, the group will remain on the path it has chosen. In an FMC, relationships with each other are founded on a trust that each member will be committed to the process and to each other. This more familiar trust has the potential for a larger trust of the mysterious process of what could possibly happen when a collection of colleagues and friends let go of prescribed outcomes and expectations.

~◦◦~

All the buried seeds
crack open in the dark
the instant they surrender
to a process they can't see.
This innate surrender
allows everything edible
and fragrant
to break ground
into a life of light
that we call Spring.
As a seed buried in the earth cannot imagine itself as an orchid or hyacinth,
neither can a heart packed with hurt imagine itself loved or at peace.
The courage of the seed is that once cracking, it cracks all the way.

Mark Nepo, "All the Buried Seeds"

For Conversation and Reflection

1. Describe an experience in which you allowed yourself to trust the process that encouraged a seed in your life to crack open.
2. Sometimes we trust ourselves but not others and the circumstances. Or sometimes we trust others and the circumstances

more than we trust ourselves. When we mistrust ourselves, others, or the circumstances, we often move into patterns of control that are signaled by pushing or holding back. Are you more inclined toward a pattern of trusting yourself, or trusting others, or neither?

3. What do you implicitly trust in yourself at this time? Describe how this trust manifests itself on a daily basis.

4. Reflect on an issue in your life or work that you are either pushing against or holding back from allowing yourself to trust.

5. In what ways does trust play a role in your scholarship, teaching, and service?

Diversity

In the natural world, a homogeneous population often is unhealthy and unsustainable. Today's farmers typically rely on fertilizers and pesticides to fight the diseases and other issues that emerge with massive fields of corn. In contrast, the Iroquois centuries ago found that corn flourished when grown in combination with beans and squash. These "three sisters" not only provided a bountiful harvest, but each contributed to the development of the others. Beans climbed the tall corn plant to capture the sun while making each corn stalk more resilient to the wind even as the low, broad squash leaves kept the soil moist for all three plants.

Diversity is also a condition for human growth and flourishing. Research on college students, for example, consistently demonstrates that racially diverse educational environments are associated with positive intellectual and personal outcomes.[5] Meaningful engagement across differences exposes people to multiple perspectives and challenges preconceived notions. Over time, experiences with diversity often contribute to people developing greater capacities for critical thinking and empathy, among many other outcomes. Like the Iroquois's three sisters, people flourish best in relation to diverse others, each contributing to and benefiting from the variety within the group.

Diversity manifests in many ways on our campuses and in FMCs. Whereas we typically think of diversity in terms of race, class, and gender, within an FMC, different aspects of a person's identity might be more or less salient at different times. In one FMC, age became a central consideration when the members discussed what it means for an academic to be "productive." And they all learned from a sustained discussion of work-life balance with people in the group who ranged from a married woman with adult children to a young, single gay man. Although these discussions did not lead to perfect work-life balance for any of them, they left the conversations with additional empathy and respect for each other and with a renewed understanding of an area of common struggle.

Exploring diverse aspects of our individual and group identities can be uncomfortable for some on campus, including FMC participants. Groups should approach these and all other topics with care, allowing time and conversation to build the trust necessary for deep engagement. Group members also should remember that the group does not need to come to consensus for all to learn and grow. As David Bohm explains, dialogue is most valuable when it exposes beliefs and thoughts rather than when it produces a neat resolution.[6] Dialogue might be frustrating or even contentious, but with a community of trust and respect, it ultimately produces deeper understanding.

One starting point for cultivating diversity as a condition for growth is recognizing that as colleagues in higher education, FMC members speak a common language of academic discourse. Yet each individual also brings a multitude of voices to the group based on our many affiliations. Each of us is a host of diversity unto ourselves, with diverse ways of speaking, thinking, and making sense of our lives. Taking the time to shed the habits of speaking in academic discourse and letting the many possible voices be heard will open the group toward possibilities usually shut down in the university. Doing so may help to bridge the fragmentation between public and private personas, inviting a more unified, whole self to be heard.

In fostering diversity within the FMCs, we have discovered the richness that comes from bringing in a variety of points of view, which in turn generates creativity and surprising opportunities that can contribute to the common good.

~☯~

The World does not stay attached to a particular invention. It seeks diversity. It wants to move on to more inventing, to more possibilities. The world's desire for diversity compels us to change.

Margaret J. Wheatley and Myron Kellner-Rogers, A Simpler Way

For Conversation and Reflection

1. Spend time going beyond the habits of "academic speak" to open the space for diverse patterns of speech and expression specific to participants' backgrounds.

2. Reflect on larger patterns and habits in your life relating to diversity. What are the communities of diversity of which you are a member?

3. Diversity is itself diverse; that is, there is more than one kind of diversity. Reflect on the varieties of diversity that have an impact on your life and work.

4. Describe specific ways in which you may have participated in a monocultural community and what effects that may have had on your perspectives.

5. In what areas within your work have you experienced the gifts that others bring to the table? What were the conditions that catalyzed or fostered that exchange?

Humility

Formation mentoring communities are fed by the reality that we don't know the answers. Imagine that a group of academics gathered together without pretense of certitude. In FMCs, we join with colleagues to begin a journey without knowing where we are going, not knowing what we may gain together, or what rewards lie at the end of the journey. But something happens along the way when we choose open-mindedness and curiosity over protecting our point of view. When we approach situations from a perspective of humility, possibilities open. We spend more time in that wonderful space of the beginner's mind, willing to learn from what others have to offer. We forget about being perfect and enjoy being in the moment. The formation mentoring process begins with questions, not necessarily with the answers, which, for Rilke, "cannot be given to you, because you would not be able to live them. And the point is, to live everything. Live the questions now. Perhaps, you will then gradually, without noticing it, live along some distant day into the answer."[7]

Indeed, humility is countercultural, even radical, in higher education. FMCs provide a space to nurture such radical ways of being. They are counterpoints to the academy's tradition of distinguishing and honoring by virtue of rank, tenure, status, achievement, honors, and awards. Instead, FMCs seek to level relationships, putting aside the member's respective rank, status, power, and exclusive standings in the institution. Thus, humility is indispensable to the development and sustenance of an FMC.

But we should not confuse humility with diffidence or faint-heartedness. Humility is not about concealing ourselves with a veneer of false modesty or self-deprecation. It includes the truth about who we are, our achievements, our worth—but without self-importance or arrogance. It is the antithesis of raw ambition and hubris. Humility calls for an unobtrusive confidence, without the need for a specious selling of our accomplishments. It's about being content to let others discover the stratums of our selves without having to self-aggrandize. Engaging in conversation with humility does not mean that we lack determination or do not try to excel; however, it does require doing away with arrogance. In some cultures, humility is considered an expression of being in the true nature or in balance of the middle way.

Humility means understanding that the joys, pains, desires, and needs of others are as worthy as our own. When we are humble, we can laugh at our sense of self-importance and sometimes simply set it on the shelf. We can see our own faults and the strengths of others, and we can recognize how much we have been given. Humility makes us aware of our personal limitations and the limitations of humanity more broadly. We can acknowledge that there is much we do not know and that with many things, certainty is impossible and that our understandings of the world are provisional at best. Humility is also a virtue that cross-fertilizes into other key conditions for growth. For example, maintaining a hospitable space requires a degree of humility among the group and its members because each must ensure that there is sufficient space for everyone to be present and to be heard. In addition, a habit of being humble within a safe space makes it more likely that members may allow themselves to be vulnerable within the group, and thus be more open to personal formation.

Let us not forget that the root word of humility is *humus*, "brought to earth." Humility, then, is fertile soil from which we may grow. It keeps our ears to the ground of possibility. It quiets the noise of our own ego, creating a space that might allow the alchemy of conversation to give birth to new directions and surprising paths, individually or collectively.

~◎~

Not the bristle-bearded Igors bent
under burlap sacks, not peasants knee-deep
in the rice-paddy muck,
nor the serfs whose quarter-moon sickles
make the wheat fall in waves
they don't get to eat. My friend the Franciscan
nun says we misread
that word meek in the Bible verse that blesses them.
To understand the meek
(she says) picture a great stallion at full gallop
in a meadow, who—
at his master's voice—seizes up to a stunned
but instant halt.
So with the strain of holding that great power
in check, the muscles
along the arched neck keep eddying,
and only the velvet ears
prick forward, awaiting the next order.

Mary Karr, "Who the Meek Are Not"

For Conversation and Reflection

1. How does a sense of humility allow you to listen more attentively and respond more thoughtfully to what you have heard?

2. Describe moments of the presence of humility in yourself and others.

3. Share an experience of where an act of humility opened you to growth and love.

4. Reflect on a time when arrogance shut down a dialogue or an opportunity for growth.

5. Identify instances where you have witnessed acts of humility in higher education. What role does humility play in your discipline? How might your collegial relationships be transformed through acts of humility?

Accountability

In the context of higher education, accountability most often refers to evaluative measures used to determine whether students, faculty, and administrators are meeting standards agreed on by the institution or outside accrediting agencies. Yet as with many other terms we use in this book, there is a more expansive meaning of the word *accountability* that we wish to recapture. We are considering not only how we are accountable for our actions as professionals, but also how we are accountable to one another and accountable to ourselves for working toward our own personal aspirations. In this sense, accountability is about the way in which we stand next to each other, serving as reminders, guides, and support as we journey toward our intentions, callings, and goals.

In our FMCs, we find ourselves expressing desires about who we want to become and how we would like to change. We discuss ways that we could grow in the context of a single challenging situation, in the short term of a single semester, or in the long term of our entire career. One member remarks that she has forgotten how much more alive she feels when spending time outdoors; another says he has creative projects that have been waiting in the wings for years, and if he doesn't focus on them soon, they will wither on the vine; and another realizes that he has to shed various administrative roles because he has less and less time for students.

FMC members listen to the resonance of these stories; we remember them, and at the opportune moment, we may gently remind one another of them. We listen not only to the person who is speaking but to the person who is being aspired toward. FMC members agree to hold each other accountable to these aspirations. Periodically one person in the group may ask others these questions: "When was the last time you went outside?" "Have you been making time for your creative projects as you said you would?" "How have you focused your energies so that you can devote more time for your students?"

These questions are asked without condemnation or judgment and instead in a way to help recall the other person to her stated goals and aspirations. While other groups may require safety, honesty, and trust, it is perhaps this quality of accountability that most clearly distinguishes FMCs. Unlike many therapy groups or rap sessions, in an FMC, we are not content to simply express feelings and familiar issues; we create lasting relationships in which fellow members encourage us to lead the lives and engage in the acts we aspire to. En*courage*ment, we should remind ourselves, is no small matter; it is the working of the heart toward greater intentions. Accountability, as we are applying this term to FMCs, is the antidote to superficiality or stagnation in group interactions. It is an essential ingredient for the work of formation.

Academics accept as a matter of course that they will be held accountable to standards and deadlines, to policies and proce-dures. But what of being held accountable to another person, a colleague, or a group of colleagues? That would require a personal commitment; it would require giving something of ourselves, which we may be reluctant to do. Furthermore, the typical campus setting does not offer faculty or staff sufficient opportunities to enter into such relationships of accountability and trust. The development of FMCs on campus has the potential to change that.

Formation mentoring community group members place their trust in each other, and there exists a reasonable expectation that they will all be faithful to that trust. In our experience, fidelity—to the FMC group and the others in the group—is one of the essential conditions for mentoring, formation, and growth to occur in this community context. Showing up on time, being present, listening generously, holding one another accountable, maintaining the agreed-on practices of the group: all of these are small but significant and necessary acts of fidelity. They are ways of keeping faith with the other members of the community to which we, of our own free initiative, have now committed ourselves and to which we therefore belong.

It is important to recall that accountability, as we are presenting it, is not about meeting a particular standard set by some outside entity. No one in the FMC is going to put you on probation if you fail to meet some standard of growth. The others are not hired to swoop in, examine you, write up a list of citations, and send the report six months later. Rather, the others are co-cultivators of your best self. Something remarkable happens when a group of people makes this sort of commitment to one another: we begin to reflect not just ourselves back to one another, but the selves that we aspire to become. In such a circle of friends, we know that we are much less alone in this world, and that when acting in concert for mutual growth, we are more likely to engage in sustained personal formation.

The people I love the best
jump into work head first
without dallying in the shallows
and swim off with sure strokes almost out of sight.
They seem to become natives of that element,
the black sleek heads of seals
bouncing like half-submerged balls.

I love people who harness themselves, an ox to a heavy cart,
who pull like water buffalo, with massive patience,
who strain in the mud and the muck to move things forward,
who do what has to be done, again and again.

I want to be with people who submerge
in the task, who go into the fields to harvest
and work in a row and pass the bags along,
who are not parlor generals and field deserters
but move in a common rhythm
when the food must come in or the fire be put out

The work of the world is common as mud.
Botched, it smears the hands, crumbles to dust.
But the thing worth doing well done
has a shape that satisfies, clean and evident.
Greek amphoras for wine or oil,
Hopi vases that held corn, are put in museums
but you know they were made to be used.
The pitcher cries for water to carry
and a person for work that is real.

Marge Piercy, "To be of use"

For Conversation and Reflection

1. Describe an aspiration or quality of character to which you would like to be encouraged and to be held accountable.

2. Are you ready to be reminded by others of the goals and aspirations that you have set for yourself? How can you make yourself more receptive to the mentoring that will occur in an FMC?

3. Holding each other accountable can be uncomfortable. There is no one right way or right choice of words to broach sensitive issues. Discuss with FMC members what sort of language you would be most receptive to when you are being held accountable.

4. Reflect on instances in which family and friends have held you accountable, or vice versa. How have these examples resulted in personal formation?

5. Think about ways in which this type of expanded accountability could spill over into more traditional, professional notions of accountability. Are there ways in which you are more accountable to your students as a result of FMC conversations?

Friendship

Sociological research suggests that we may be losing the art of developing and sustaining friendships today. A widely reported study published in the *American Sociological Review* in June 2006 replicated a study done twenty-five years earlier.[8] Researchers at the University of Arizona and Duke University asked participants, selected randomly from the general American public, to give the first name or initials of all the people, including family members, with whom they discussed "important matters." In 1985 respondents had on average three such people; in 2006 respondents had on average only two. Also in 2006, 25 percent of respondents indicated

57

that they had no one in their lives with whom they could discuss important matters. A quarter of the population had no friends, confidants, or close family members. Other studies have documented the diminishing of social capital over the past generation, as summarized in Robert Putnam's book, *Bowling Alone.*[9]

Although we do not have specific data in this regard, we can probably assume that these national trends apply equally to people on our college campuses, perhaps even more than among the general population. In an age where "to friend" has become a verb to link people, many of whom we will never meet face to face, into a social network, we have to reflect for a moment on the nature of our friendships. How many genuine friends do you count among your colleagues on campus? While you may share mutual intellectual or professional interests with many, are there some for whom there is a real, mutual bond of affection? Are there specific obstacles on today's campuses or in our wider culture that make collegial friendships even less likely to develop or more difficult to sustain? While our connectivity has become broader—we have a huge list of contacts available on our "smart phones" at the touch of a button—our connectedness to them might be shallower.

Most readers would probably agree that engaging in meaningful professional work is part and parcel of the pursuit of happiness, part of our efforts to fulfill our potential and purpose. As mentioned in chapter 1, Aristotle's *Nichomachean Ethics* is built around questions about what makes human beings flourish. He begins with a discussion of happiness and virtue in books I to VII. The capstone of the work, in books IX and XIII, is a consideration of friendship. It may seem strange to many modern readers that a book on human flourishing, happiness, ethics, and virtue suddenly shifts gears at the end with an apparently peripheral essay on friendship. But for Aristotle, the transition was seamless. He understood both contemplation and friendship as necessary for our happiness; friendship was precisely the context in which the virtues he previously described were developed and lived. Friendship was among the preeminent conditions for human growth.

Aristotle distinguished three types of friendship: the first two were an imperfect form, and the third was friendship in the truest sense. He called the first imperfect type the friendship of utility. This is where the other is loved because he or she is somehow useful to us. Many collegial and business relationships are built on this thin foundation. We develop a certain sort of relationship with a colleague so that he or she will write us a good letter of recommendation and so forth.

The second type of imperfect friendship he called friendship of pleasure. This is a relationship in which the other person is loved because he or she is pleasant or agreeable to us. We like hanging around Professor Smith in the faculty lounge because she makes us laugh. Aristotle noted that these two types of friendships are easily dissolved: when one person ceases to be useful (the final grant report is submitted) or pleasant (Smith is not telling any jokes anymore), the friendship fades. Their foundations are not enduring. All of us likely have plenty of these relationships. They are friends of a certain sort, perhaps more accurately described as casual friends, buddies, or acquaintances. Aristotle did not denigrate these relationships or advise that we try to develop all of our imperfect friendships into perfect friendships. One has many acquaintances but only so much time.

But for those others with whom we have deeper connections, it is worth every effort to develop what Aristotle called "perfect" friendship: true friendship, genuine friendship. At the center of this friendship is *philia*—love that involves not only affection but concrete acts of the will. We not only want our friends to be happy and to flourish, but we act in ways to help bring this about.

Genuine friendship requires habits of the heart, character strengths, and virtues.

You might respond at this point: I already have old friends from college, friends in the neighborhood, or a group of friends from church. Do I need friends at work, at the university? Will that contribute to my productivity or distract me from my real priorities? Perhaps those are not the right questions to ask ourselves.

⟳ *From Our FMCs*

Perhaps Less Is More

On my way from one of our group's sessions, I spotted an advertisement for a Web browser. It showed a sea of people staring up at a billboard, which read: "It's time for a new kind of community (pop. 400,000,000+)." It occurred to me that my colleagues and I are convinced, rather, that it's time for a new kind of community (pop. 4+).

But if it is through our relationships that we create and sustain culture, then what is happening on our campuses when genuine friendships among faculty and staff become scarcer and scarcer? What does it mean when we are proud of our connectivity with 400 million but forget our connectedness to 4?

One of the most significant and unexpected gifts of FMCs is that they have turned out to be places that cultivate friendships. The conditions set in FMCs diminish the tendency toward imperfect friendships of utility and pleasure that Aristotle described. They are not structured around utility (being productive and getting something done) or grounded in just pleasure or pleasantries (drinking or golfing together). An FMC creates the conditions for friendship by cultivating the virtues and habits of the heart that expand our capacity for friendship: hospitality, safety, courage, honesty, trust, diversity, humility, and accountability.

In an FMC, the rhythm of regular meetings over time creates a shared history and an anticipated future—the time and familiarity that are the water and sunlight for the growth of friendship. One need not form friendships with all the participants in one's mentoring group; time and circumstances may not allow this. But if no friendships developed among group members, one would have to wonder whether the FMC was functioning in a manner consistent with its purpose. It seems to us that this is one way in which FMCs can augment the social capital on our campuses and help reverse some of the trends in our culture that have led to diminished lives.

Engaging in conversations about these issues provides fertile ground out of which more perfect friendships can emerge.

~ⓐ~

Stay together friends
Don't scatter and sleep.
Our friendship is made
Of being awake.

Rumi, Excerpted from "The Waterwheel"

For Conversation and Reflection

1. After considering Aristotle's taxonomy of friendships, discuss the individuals in your life who fall into these categories. Are there acquaintances you might anticipate could develop into a more perfect friendship in the Aristotelian sense?
2. While having more "perfect" friendships seems like a worthy goal, are there aspects of a deeper, genuine friendship that make you hesitant and uncomfortable? Why?

3. What aspects of yourself unfold in the presence of friendship? Think of ways that you have grown significantly because of a friendship.

4. Describe the characteristics and personal strengths or weaknesses that you bring to a friendship. In what ways do you experience yourself as a good friend?

5. Describe and discuss the qualities that you seek out in friendships. Why are these important for your life?

Is There a Place for Me in a Formation Mentoring Community?

ঞ

Perhaps you are new to higher education and beginning your career as a new faculty member, advisor, or administrator. Your days are full, and you may already be engaged in a mentoring process with a senior faculty member. You may be wondering what a formation mentoring community (FMC) has to offer to you.

Or perhaps your position is in administration, and although you might welcome the opportunity to be in an FMC, you might be skeptical about a mentoring community made up of staff and faculty. You might be wondering if there is a place for someone like you.

To answer those legitimate concerns, we offer the following reflections of Darris Means, a young administrator who came to the

Elon University group with many of the same kinds of questions and found the following answers:

⟿⟿⟳⟵

I was invited to participate in the formation group during the summer of 2010. I was hesitant to join the group when I learned that it would be comprised of all faculty members, and I would be the only staff member participating in the group. I was also hesitant about the time commitment; I was about to embark on my Ph.D. journey part time while working full time at the university. Could I relate to faculty members? Did I have the time to do this formation group? The idea also seemed strange to me. We would meet throughout the academic year and just talk about questions that are important to our lives and work. No agenda, no checklists, no learning objectives, and no major assignments. I had been working in higher education for only three years at the time, and I had never heard of anything like this.

I decided to take a leap of faith and accept the invitation to join the group. As I reflect back on the journey with my formation group, I know that it was one of the best decisions I made in my early career. I began in the group lost and overwhelmed in a noisy world. I was trying to be too many things to too many people, and I had forgotten who I was along the way. I did not give myself the space to contemplate my connectedness with others—family members, colleagues, friends, or students.

Although I was not always the most talkative person in the group, I left each lunch with my formation group reflecting on my journey and how I could be a better advisor, friend, brother, and student without getting lost in a noisy world. The group pointed out ideas I had never considered and provided me with opportunities to consider big questions and ideas.

The most important thing the group gave me was the space to delve deep into a journey of finding my authentic self. I'm by no means done with my journey, but each day I feel less and less overwhelmed by to-do lists, schedules, and the pressure to say yes to everything. I feel like I have more freedom than I did two years ago; I now feel like I have the power and courage to steer my journey to discovering my authentic self.

64

CHAPTER 3

The Basics of Creating Formation Mentoring Communities on Your Campus

In this chapter, we explain and describe the basic, practical aspects of creating and sustaining formation mentoring communities (FMCs). We are writing here for those who have little or no experience initiating or structuring these kinds of groups (it's the information that we wish we had when we were starting out). Those with more experience may want to skim or even skip this chapter.

Our purpose here is not to prescribe the content of what occurs in any given FMC. The topics or themes of any meeting will be as diverse as the groups themselves, and that is as it should be. The FMC should be an open space where participants fill in the content as appropriate to their concerns and circumstances.

Although we offer advice based on our collective and individual experiences of participating in an FMC for two years, we want to make it clear that creating and maintaining an FMC is extraordinarily simple. You do not need permission from anyone; there is no need for a budget; there are no minutes, no articulated outcomes, no product. This is not a rigid process but a highly local, specific, and organic one. Basically, all that is needed is the shared hunger for a deeper conversation among companions and colleagues.

Addressing Obstacles

Despite all our reassuring words, you may still have a natural and understandable hesitancy to take the first step and convene an FMC. Doing something new and different can be daunting because it involves stepping out of a comfort zone. We admit we found parts of this process challenging as well; as we have said, we weren't naturals at this. To be honest, we had plenty of questions and doubts along the way. But we can tell you that each obstacle was much more difficult in anticipation than in actuality. We learned that with each invitation, people were open and willing, putting our fears to rest. Here are our four greatest perceived obstacles and what we learned in getting past them.

Feeling Awkward

When a colleague heard of our success with FMCs, he considered creating one of his own. But he was hesitant: "I'm fearful, and I feel awkward about how to initiate the process. Part of this is simply mustering the courage to ask folks to join in a more personal endeavor—as if personal things are not part of the university and admitting, heaven forbid, that I have a personal life."

This is a familiar sentiment, one each of us felt as we made the commitment to form an FMC. Would we be seen as crossing a boundary into people's private spaces? Would we be perceived as weak, nonacademic, and too touchy-feely? But as with many other such experiences, the anxiety dissipated as soon as we began to offer the invitations, for we discovered that people are ready for this: everyone we approached to join an FMC has expressed gratitude for the invitation. We all were hungrier than we realized. Why not be nourished in good company?

Finding the Right Words

Perhaps one of the reasons individuals seized the opportunity of participating in an FMC was the nature and careful shaping of the invitation. Before extending the invitation, we reflected on the individual and the particular campus context. The colleague mentioned previously expressed further hesitance in issuing an invitation because "it also involves possessing a developed idea of a formation mentoring community and feeling as if I'll be foisting it on others." We encouraged him to use the words that he and his colleagues would be most comfortable with.

We all sought to shape our invitations and descriptions of the FMCs in ways that came naturally to us and would resonate with those we were inviting. We decided that if the notion of formation, for example, required too much explanation, it did not have to be used. But if the concepts of formation or transformation have a particular resonance, as they did for Ed and his colleagues, then they should be used.

In speaking in his particular context as a fellow junior faculty member, Aaron focused on the possible benefits of mentoring one another. Dirksen described the group as a potential community where they would wish and work toward what is best for each other, where they could have conversations about personal and professional lives that do not normally take place among colleagues. There is no right way to pitch the invitation other than thinking about the individual receiving it. Ask yourself which of the many features of FMCs would be the most salient and craft an invitation that works for you. Remember that you're offering them something they're probably searching for, even if they can't articulate it yet.

◦◦◦ *From Our FMCs*

Some People Are Ready

To plant the initial seed for the invitation, I began with a brief e-mail indicating that I wanted to talk to this person when he had a few minutes about possibly having him join a group of junior faculty to mentor one another. The next time our paths crossed was on our way to a monthly meeting of clerkship directors. I had a few minutes with him, so I figured it was either now or in another three months.

"Do you have a minute?" I asked as I pulled him aside. "You remember that thing I mentioned in the e-mail a few months ago about our mentoring group?" He stared at me blankly without saying anything. Then he pointed to his mouth and, in a garbled voice, indicated that he had just returned from the dentist. Apparently some serious work had been done on his teeth: his face did look rather swollen, and his speech when he said the word *dentist* was slurred. "I can't weally tawk wight now, but I will wisten" he said.

Well, this was awkward. But I launched in, doing my best to explain to him the why and wherefore of this group, what the group was and was not, why this was not just another hour-long committee meeting that he should try to cram onto his calendar, and so on. When I was done, not knowing whether he comprehended or connected with a single word I had said, I asked whether it sounded like something he wanted to participate in. To my surprise, without any questions, and without

---

even a "let me think about it and I'll get back to you," he simply nodded his head yes.

What did I learn from this less-than-ideal invitation? I saw that some people are just ready and that those who are ready—and we believe that such people are legion—do not need a long-winded or well-rehearsed sales pitch. They just need someone with a bit of pluck to venture toward them and give them a bit of news. If we toss such people a brief message in a bottle, a simple invitation that speaks to their predicament, they will respond naturally and readily.

My colleague did not need to be convinced or cajoled. He just needed to have me extend a friendly hand and say, "Come with me. You look a bit thirsty, and I happen to know that there is some fresh water in the cove around that corner."

Finding the Time

Time. There is never enough of it to go around. How can we possibly fit in the time around all of our other professional duties and obligations? How do we find time for each student and each of her questions? How do we find time for colleagues or, that matter, for ourselves? With our calendars filling up weeks in advance, well-intentioned faculty, administrators, and staff find it difficult to meet the needs of students and colleagues who hunger for a different type of conversation. Given this perennial predicament, how can we advocate for adding another standing meeting to the calendar? Indeed, the time commitment of an FMC is not to be taken lightly. As we discuss below, a commitment to showing up is foundational to the success of an FMC. At first, it was indeed challenging for most of us to find the time for our FMC to meet on a consistent basis. Yet we discovered that when we were able find an hour or ninety minutes every other week or once a month and take the time to reflect, discuss, and listen to others regularly, something deeply counterintuitive happened: making the time for these groups paradoxically seemed to create more time. We found through our FMC conversations that we became more discerning about our priorities and could alter the quality of the time and attention devoted to work and responsibilities.

If we continue to follow the logic that time and space are constant, measurable entities defined by their scarcity and limits, we will never be able to fit everything in. But if we step back and reflect, we may see that Einstein was right—not just in the physics of time but that our embodied experience of time is indeed relative, depending on the care we take with it.

～⁓ *From Our FMCs*

Taking Time to Make Time

From participating in our FMC, I find myself better able to swashbuckle effectively through the thickets of distractions and hone in on the stressed-out student in my office, the curriculum proposal, or the conference paper. I am able to be more discerning in my use of time, because I have reflected on my priorities and am clearer about what truly is deserving of the best of my time. The next meeting I have with a student in my office takes on a different tone, a deeper listening, with echoes of the history and the promise of the future of education. If we take the time to be reminded of our calling we are more likely to answer it.

Joining Yet Another Group

Many are drawn to higher education because of the degree of independence the work appears to afford. Yet we are often called into group work that is complicated and task oriented: governance, committee work, task forces, councils, research groups, and such.

Isolation or, worse, strained professional relationships lead to burnout and a sense of widespread discontent. A recent review article in the *Chronicle of Higher Education* concluded that higher education faculty now suffer burnout at increasingly high rates: "The days when academia was a low-stress working environment are over, with 'burnout' levels now comparable with those in other service sectors." The study concluded that a growing number of academics experience "the depletion of emotional reserves (emotional exhaustion), an increasingly cynical and negative approach towards others (depersonalization) and a growing feeling of work-related dissatisfaction."[1]

So the thought of joining another group will likely bring images of the same taxing work disguised as restorative, another commitment that drains our diminishing resources of energy and spirit. Yet we discovered that though we cringed at the idea of another meeting or committee, these groups created a different kind of community that actually enriched all of our other work. They were not a taxing drain, but a chance to renew and refresh our energies. We found also that they provided necessary support for our work: we can seek the wisdom of those in our FMCs even apart from the specific time we have designated for the meeting. When we need another pair of eyes to help us see through the fog, FMC colleagues are often there for us.

Starting an FMC

Convening an FMC is not the same as calling a meeting. Your job isn't to set the agenda and guarantee that specific outcomes are achieved. Instead, your fundamental tasks are to bring people together, lightly but clearly structure the first few gatherings, and then support the group in charting its own path. Convening is about beginning with purpose but providing space for the group to develop as it will. Ultimately, convening a group is an opportunity for you to form a small community of individuals who are committed to learn from and with each other in order to enhance personal and professional growth.

∾⊘∽ *From Our FMCs*

You Can Do It

If I can initiate a formation mentoring community, anybody can. I am not one normally given to habits of deep conversation, contemplation, and reflection. I pretty much move through the world with a sort of abandon, not looking back unless some-one tells me I should do so. But I now hunger for the biweekly FMC gatherings, like bells rung in a monastery, reminding me of why I am here, in this place called the academy, with these other people—students, colleagues, friends. Together with my FMC companions, we deepen our purpose in our work and our lives—a large payoff for a small investment of time and energy.

Reflecting on Your Goals and Aspirations

Starting an FMC might seem daunting, but the steps are quite straightforward. Regardless of whether you are starting a group on your own or with another colleague, begin by reflecting on your aspirations for the FMC. This will help you clarify your goals and give you clues about the types of people you might want to invite to be in the group. In preparation, you might ask yourself:

- What are my hopes and intentions for this group?
- Who on campus might share similar hopes or intentions?
- What experiences and knowledge can I draw on to start this group? What might others bring to the group to enrich it?
- Am I willing to initially convene and later let go of control of the group?

You do not need to have certainty about your answers to these questions. Instead, your reflections can serve as something of a road map, allowing you to more confidently find your way to the first group meeting.

Choosing Group Members

One of the important aspects of FMCs is that they provide a rare space and time to gather together for conversation and build relationships with colleagues. FMCs do not include students but rather are drawn from your professional peers: faculty, staff, and administrators.

Your choice of group members will vary based on your context and your goals. Do you have existing relationships that you would like to deepen, or will this be an opportunity to connect with peers with whom you aren't yet linked? Do you want to stay close to your disciplinary or professional home, or would you like your FMC to reach beyond the established boundaries on campus? We suggest that whatever composition you choose, the group should have a common thread to begin with—something that might weave members together, however loosely, when they first meet.

Aaron initially invited three colleagues from within his academic department to form a group. All were relative newcomers to the medical faculty, so they shared somewhat similar positions in their careers and personal lives. Prior to forming the FMC, they rarely had the opportunity to interact meaningfully with each other about topics beyond patient care.

Peter's group began with five individuals from different parts of campus: a student life professional, an academic administrator, and faculty members from art, education, and Spanish. This group did not share a professional affiliation, the members varied widely in age, and some had to be introduced to each other at the first meeting, but all five had a strong commitment to student learning and development.

∿❧ *From Our FMCs*

Who to Invite?

When we originally agreed to convene an FMC on our four campuses, I knew immediately who I would invite—two former graduate students in my program who had become colleagues and collaborators on various projects. Both of these colleagues would be eager, I knew, for a more expansive discussion, and they would be ripe for mutual mentoring at a time when they would be considering future directions, professionally and personally.

Beyond that, it was unclear. The three of us frequently deliberated on who we might invite and how many should be in the group. An uncomfortable feeling of being exclusionary and cliquish kept us from making progress.

We considered issues of who would be committed to participating in the FMC. Who would be able to speak openly about more than work? Who would not be cynical? Who would add the right balance of diversity of backgrounds and experiences? Gender was also an issue. In the beginning, there were two men and one woman. We felt it was important to have a balance. Ultimately we decided on two younger faculty members, one from art and the other from theater.

As you weigh the possibilities for your group, you might want to:

- Consider what relationships already exist between possible group members. Some FMCs build effectively on prior connections, allowing members to dive more deeply into conversation quickly; however, the nature and habits of these relationships might color the FMC, particularly if some members are friends or disciplinary colleagues while others are not. Other FMCs can begin with people who might not know each other. This can help to create openness and allow people to join on equal footing, although it might mean the group starts more slowly as relationships and trust are established.

- Consider the career stage of possible group members. Relatively new faculty and staff often are eager for connections and meaningful conversation. More experienced colleagues might be ready to deepen or renew their aspirations. FMCs with members at different career stages need to take care not to fall into common campus habits of veterans advising newcomers, but this diversity might also add depth and enrich the group's conversation.

- Consider people who seem ripe for this type of conversation. In all four of our campuses, we found people eager to join our groups. Look for people you suspect would see this opportunity as a welcome gift. You might not know them well, but perhaps you once lingered with them after a committee meeting to share a story, or perhaps you regularly see someone at discussions about a topic that interests you. They are out there if you look.

- Give some consideration to factors like gender, ethnicity, departmental affiliation, or other aspects of individual identity. Higher education has been plagued by the paradox of institutions that stand for the pursuit of truth, freedom, justice, and equality and yet continue to be places where many struggle to survive and thrive. Some FMCs might benefit from members who are similar in certain salient ways, while other groups might be enlivened by differences. Your context and goals should inform your choices about what aspects of diversity or commonality you want in your FMC.

- To ensure the level of trust and honesty needed for transformative conversations, all members must carry equal weight within the FMC. It is worth noting here that if someone is going to have a primary role in the evaluation or rank and promotion process of another, the two should not be in the same group. All faculty eventually may vote on each other, but if, for example, a person is going to write the up-or-down recommendation, some of what she might have gleaned in an FMC could bear in a very direct way on the recommendation. (For more on this, see "Creating a Level Playing Field" in chapter 4.)

These considerations might make the process of starting a group seem overwhelmingly complex, but they need not be. We raise these issues simply to encourage some deliberate reflection on the foundation you are constructing for your group. Ironically, our core group of six (that is, the four authors and our two mentors) first came together around the concept of formation mentoring, yet the actual makeup of our group was hardly intentional. The fact that we were four men with two female mentors was not by design, nor was our disciplinary and institutional variation based on any plan. Yet we found the randomness of our convening allowed important matters of diversity to emerge. Through the past four years, we have learned to attend to what we have in common and what differentiates us. The diversity within our group, and the unlikely situation that brought us together, have been positive factors, stimulating creativity rather than being obstacles to formation. Thus, we encourage you to develop your group thoughtfully, but also to recognize that serendipity may play a role in your experience.

The Invitation

Once you think through whom you would like to invite to participate in the FMC, the next step is to solicit participation. We each chose to convene our groups by personal invitation, outside the formal structures of our institutions. We found that explaining the purpose and process of FMCs seemed to require face-to-face conversations. In the course of the invitation, we emphasized that individuals were free to join the group or to pass. We wanted our busy colleagues to elect to participate rather than to feel obligated to join. Perhaps most important, we wanted the group to be co-constructed from the start. Although we were initially acting as the convener of our groups, each of us made it clear that this was not to be "my" group; it would be "ours." To create that shared sense of belonging and ownership, we asked our colleagues to help lay the group's foundation.

Peter wanted to form a group that developed a strong sense of purpose, yet without the expectation that the group would be productive in some conventionally academic way: producing research, improving our teaching, or becoming more efficient and effective. But given that we all spend so much time trying to achieve, he imagined that his colleagues might feel uncomfortable spending time trying simply to be together. He wondered what the response would be to such an invitation. Was it responsible, he wondered, to invite pretenure colleagues into such a group, or would he potentially be undermining that person's professional progress? On a campus characterized by a culture of busyness, would colleagues really go for such a fuzzy and apparently nonproductive idea? And could he justify making such a commitment when he already felt stretched thin at work and wanted more time for his life beyond campus?

To articulate his aspirations and raise these questions, he decided that he needed to have an individual conversation with each potential group member. He sent a brief e-mail to each of the peers he had identified, asking them to lunch to talk about a potential project. At the face-to-face lunch meetings, he explained his hopes for the group and his reasons for inviting that individual to join it. He welcomed their questions, concerns, and ideas. Although these conversations became quite animated, he told each colleague that he didn't expect or want the person to commit to the group during that lunch. He promised to follow up with an e-mail a couple of days later, inviting questions and further conversation. Each of his follow-up e-mails received a prompt and enthusiastic positive response.

At the University of Washington, Ed had a different approach. He arranged time to talk with each member he considered inviting to the FMC. He asked questions, probing their comfort and his own comfort with core ideas related to formation mentoring. With Jim, Ed asked, "What is your reaction to the whole notion of formation?" He wrote to Ed later that day and said that transformation was likely a concept he was more comfortable with in his own teaching, that is, the discovery of how people journey through this life and the ideas, people, critical moments, that shape and transform the way we engage in the world.

They discussed what texts might help inform the FMC's discussion. Jim, classicist that he is, offered the story of Achilles, *The Odyssey, Iphigenia, Confessions of St. Augustine*, and Bill Murray's film *Groundhog Day*. Ed wondered if Malcolm X was a story of formation/transformation, or perhaps also the independent film *The Station Agent*, about how a man born with dwarfism, after losing a friend and mentor, moves to the outskirts of New Jersey to find solitude and ultimately finds friendship with three people whose lives become intertwined and connected like the very trains that inspire them.

In essence, Ed was careful in choosing who might fit with the concept of formation mentoring. He followed a similar process with each potential member. By the time they formed their FMC, he had tested the ideas, themes, and writings and had already begun creating norms for the group.

The Structure of an FMC

In contrast to a meeting, a group is more than the sum of its parts. A group has a life of its own—a personality, a heart, and perhaps even a soul. This quality allows the ideas and experiences that emerge from a group to be more than any of the members can access alone. While group dynamics have been extensively studied and documented, this elusive and expansive quality evades empirical measurements.

The Optimal Size

Group dynamics are in part a function of group size. Being in a group of thirty may cause us to say something different when we speak than what we might say in a group of four. What is less obvious is that what is said might be different in a group of three than a group of four or in a group of four than in a group of five.

In our FMCs, we have found that small groups, typically with four to six members, allow time for each individual to be heard and to listen, even during gatherings of only an hour. This size also requires each person to commit to the group and be accountable to this community. Because absence is felt, presence is vital. Although the potential for connection in very small groups can be enticing, groups that are smaller than four members may struggle to maintain momentum or generate sufficient diversity of perspective in conversations.

While we recommend small groups, larger groups can also work well. For example, Finding Meaning in Medicine, a unique conversation program for physicians and other health care professionals, functions well as a fixed small group of six to eight members but also as a drop-in group that may include as many as twenty members, recognizing that all members might not be able to attend every group meeting.[2] Over time, all members know and have joined in conversation with every other person in the group, but rarely do two meetings have the identical participants. The key to this program's success is the clear interactional agreements that all are committed to holding and carrying out. The agreements remain the same in each meeting, no matter who attends. This model can be a successful alternative to the small FMCs that we have found to be effective on our various campuses. In your context, you will need to discover the right group size to meet your goals.

Choosing the Meeting Space

We have found it helpful to select a simple, warm environment in a relatively quiet location free of disruptions. Consider also who "owns" the space and what it is that people associate with the space. Is it, for example, a meeting space, a group member's office, an eating space, or something else?

Basic comforts and conveniences are important too: accessibility, temperature, bathroom and parking accessibility, access to food or drink, and so on. It is essential that there be a sense of privacy; often this means the ability to close doors so that there are no interruptions, though one of our groups found a way to create this private space in a local restaurant. Two examples reflect some of the issues and lessons learned in choosing two very different spaces for FMCs.

Dirksen writes that at Gallaudet, they struggled with finding a home for their FMC:

⌒◜◡◝⌒

At first, we met in restaurants or pubs, but soon it became evident that this was not a wise choice for us. The noise and lack of ceremonial space made it hard to distinguish our conversation from any other good conversation in a local campus pub.

In order to break from this nomadic beginning, we met once at the Smithsonian Museum of American Art. With a newly renovated lobby, this was precisely the sort of space that engendered a sense of ceremony and contemplation. We decided we had found our space. But even after many attempts, we have not been able to return. The time and effort needed to drive, bus, walk, Metro, etc., was simply prohibitive. That is when we began a more guerrilla-type strategy of claiming space and time during the week. If we could find a moment that worked for us, we would scurry away toward the hotel and conference center on campus, grab a coffee, and talk to one another for an hour. These meetings were like recess for the mind and spirit, but the timing was sporadic and unpredictable.

Once we finally increased our group size to four, we became much more consistent and ritualized around the time and space for the meeting: every other Monday at 4:00 p.m. This way, we begin the week with an introspective discussion that sustains us throughout the weeks to come. Along with an agreed-on time, we finally settled on the perfect spot—a porch under colonnades in the nineteenth-century Chapel Hall. In this setting we have talked about contemporary issues within the setting of the history of the institution and its original mission, established in 1864.

Looking back, we see that the nomadic nature of the group was a distraction from the real business at hand: formation of ourselves in community. If I were to start over, I would seek more consistency in time and place from the beginning.

At Elon, Peter notes that a local Thai restaurant has been a source for good food and growing community:

⧸⧹

Together we've shared a few epiphanies and quite a lot of Thai food. The power and the meaning in the group come from the routine—the informal rituals of what we do. We check in with each other, spending as much time as we need to talk through the successes and struggles of the past couple of weeks. Then we talk about a theme that we've decided in advance to explore, such as productivity or community or courage. We eat. As we prepare to depart, we reconfirm what we will do together next.

The importance of that rhythm became apparent one spring when Nina spent the semester teaching in Costa Rica. Before she left, we resolved that distance wouldn't change our community or our practices of gathering together. We found a new time that seemed to work for us, although it meant we wouldn't be sharing lunch (we even talked about having Thai food delivered for our late-morning conversations!). We found a space that would allow us to Skype with Nina in private. We made a plan for what we'd discuss, and we reviewed our rules of engagement to be sure they would work in our new setting.

It didn't work. Meeting in my office to Skype was no less convenient than meeting in the Thai restaurant, but it didn't feel right. Some of us were close to the computer and more visible to Nina, while others faded into the background. The timing also didn't quite click. More often than not, someone rushed in at the last minute or ducked out before we had concluded. We couldn't sink our teeth into anything, literally or metaphorically. Our FMC had seemed strong, but it was more fragile than any of us expected when we picked it up to move it. We needed the rhythm and routine to create a space for risk taking and authenticity. And perhaps more important, we needed a space that enabled us to carve out a place where we could explore and share the small yet important choices and decisions and interactions that make up our daily lives. We couldn't plan for epiphanies, but we could create a context that could make them possible. In the end, we recommitted to resume our meetings at the Thai restaurant for lunch when Nina returned to campus.

Setting the Meeting Time

The FMC meetings should be welcome occasions, not burdensome obligations, so meetings should not be too frequent. But going too long between meetings can make it difficult for the group to have a sense of continuity and maintain the thread of ongoing conversations. The frequency should allow time for reflections to set in yet not overburden people's schedules.

We recommend meeting at least once a month. With the typical length of the academic semester, meeting less than monthly would mean just one or two meetings in a semester, which may not allow the community to sustain itself. With our FMCs, we've found that meeting twice monthly enables a group to create traction and cohesiveness more quickly.

We recommend finding some time during the workday rather than the evening to avoid conflicting with other commitments and personal obligations. Different groups set aside a midmorning hour, lunchtime, or midafternoon for their gatherings.

As to the length of the meeting session, choose a time long enough for real conversation to occur but not so long that it is impossible to attend. We have found that meeting for one to two hours works well. Consider scheduling in a bit of extra time to accommodate arrivals and departures.

There can be challenges, such as identifying a common time for all members of an FMC to meet. The Gallaudet and Elon groups found that it takes a while to gain full traction and get into a rhythm. The Gallaudet group had a sporadic meeting schedule for the first year and experienced several cancellations and postponements. It was not until the second year and the addition of a fourth member that the regularity of the meeting was established.

The Elon group had a difficult time getting steady meetings going in the first year and did not hit its stride until the second year. For this group, taking time every two weeks has made all the difference through a difficult semester. As with the Gallaudet group, the regular meeting time has now become habitual. The sooner that an agreed-on time and space is found, the sooner that traction and consistency, and then depth of discussion, may be found.

Creating the Container for Your Formation Mentoring Communities

While the content of the conversations that occur in FMCs will be as varied as the groups themselves, we have found it helpful to establish some basic norms and expectations that give the groups sufficient structure within which to operate. We refer to this as the container within which the various contents of the conversations can be placed. Some norms are applicable to all groups, while others may be adopted or discarded based on the particular needs and circumstances of the FMC. For example, the frequency or location of group meetings can vary (within reason) according to circumstances, while the norm of confidentiality is important for all FMCs.

We address the eight norms that we believe are applicable to all FMCs. After a brief discussion of these, we offer considerations regarding other norms or group agreements that an FMC might choose to adopt or adapt according to its circumstances.

Group Agreements

The initial convener can help establish the ground rules for the first meeting and those that follow. This person can model how to pay attention to the process and the time and be able to listen and help people articulate what is at issue. The content—what gets put in the container—is not the facilitator's responsibility and is not dictated by her agenda. But the container itself is something precious that she helps to create and maintain for the other group participants. This is particularly important at the beginning because the container holds the new community together and helps to establish the patterns and norms of interaction.

Elements of the Container for FMCs

1. Choose a consistent meeting space and a regular meeting time.
2. Begin and end the meeting on time.
3. Prioritize the meeting on your calendar, and show up. Attending is a commitment. (Let the convener know in advance if you cannot make a meeting or will arrive late.)
4. Practice confidentiality: what is said in the group stays in the group.
5. Listen generously and openly without interrupting the speaker.
6. Avoid dominating the conversation; leave time and space for everyone to participate.
7. Speak from personal experience without getting lost in abstract theory or academic discourse.
8. Gently remind one another of these norms if they are breached. Periodically revisit the norms and agreements as a group.[3]

In an FMC, the group does not need to have a particular leader or chairperson; each group member, including the convener or facilitator, takes responsibility for holding the container in trust.

Over time each member of the group can assume the facilitation roles. Rotating this role helps the various group members share responsibility for ensuring that the FMC is a cooperative and collegial enterprise. It also helps to establish and maintain a level playing field for all members. Thus, it is important that the container itself is described adequately and well understood by all members of the group.

Each group can also develop its own additional agreements and norms that are applicable to their situation and circumstances. These should cover the larger questions as to how the group will work together, as well as smaller issues, such as whether people can bring food to the sessions.

Attendance

Attending is a commitment: the expectation is that all members will come for each session; it is not a drop-in meeting, with people coming and going when it's convenient. Absence of members at an FMC meeting has an adverse impact on the group in terms of its depth and consistency.

Given the investment of precious time that each group member makes, respect for this commitment requires planning regular meetings ahead of time and prioritizing them on your calendar rather than organizing each meeting ad hoc. Also, the meetings should begin and end on time, and group members should make all reasonable efforts to arrive on time.

It is helpful if one member is notified in advance of who will attend so that the group knows when it is ready to begin. The group also needs to decide what happens if someone misses a gathering. Does someone e-mail those who were absent to catch them up on the theme of the day, or is this recapped at the start of the next meeting? If there are only two or three people who can attend a meeting, should the meeting be postponed or rescheduled? These are among the questions that each group needs to discuss sometime in the first few sessions.

> ◦◦ *From Our FMCs*
>
> ### Committing to the Community
>
> When I invited each member to participate in our FMC, I suggested that we begin by meeting once a month for an hour. I also suggested that such a group would likely not work unless we prioritized it and committed ourselves to the meeting time. This was really a way of committing ourselves to one another and to this shared endeavor. The small group of four simply would not work if people took a "come and go as I please" approach or showed up only when it was convenient, which, given our schedules, could mean almost never. Everyone seemed to understand this immediately, and not as a way of pressuring one another ("Show up or else!") but as a way of being available for one another. Show up because your presence is needed, because you will be missed in your absence.

Participation

Accepting the invitation to join an FMC means committing to and engaging with the others in the group. Participation is part of this commitment. Peter Block reminds us in his book, *Community: A Structure of Belonging*, that, when we bring our individual willingness to act on values, on what matters most into the collective and institutional arena, then any group will recognize that acting on what matters for one person will happen in concert with those around that person. Individual effort alone will not be enough.[4] When we manifest what is most essential to us with our peers, we create space for each individual's gifts and talents and provide room where each person is respected and appreciated.

Everyone in the FMC has a unique contribution to make. Each voice contributes to the conversation, including members who are more reserved or shy by temperament. Sometimes participation can be facilitated by simple words of encouragement from another group member: "Every time I hear you speak, you say something valuable. I would like to hear you say more." This should be done judiciously and skillfully, with naturalness. Excessive managing of contributions, especially early on as the group is forming, might feel too forced and turn people away.

The group members all have a role in encouraging participation, but also need to recognize that there are many ways to participate. The receptive mode of listening is often considered a personal failure in American culture ("If you're not talking, you're not contributing"). In an FMC, you can participate by speaking or by listening; both are valuable contributions. Angeles Arrien's cross-cultural work regarding principles of communication can contribute to our understanding of the nature of participation in an FMC. We have found her four universal communication principles helpful in guiding our work in these groups:

1. Show up and choose to be present.
2. Pay attention to what has heart and meaning.
3. Tell the truth without blame or judgment.
4. Be open to outcome, not attached to outcome.[5]

Generous Listening

In our work with FMCs, we have been deeply influenced by the concept of generous listening, an interactional technique developed by Rachel Naomi Remen and fully described in her *Finding Meaning in Medicine Resource Guide*.[6] Among other things, she suggests that conversation groups should allow silences when they occur naturally, as silence can be an opportunity for connection to self and to others. Many people are uncomfortable with periods of silence, but instead of jumping in with filler speech to break the awkward silence, we need to recognize silence as a place where we can connect to each other and to ourselves. In the context of FMC conversations, silences are not empty. Often what is said after a silence takes the conversation to another or deeper level. Sometimes silence means that people's memories have been evoked or they are integrating their own insights.

Finding Meaning in Medicine Guidelines for Conversation

- Generous listening.
- Confidentiality.
- No interruptions when someone is speaking.
- Allow for all differences.
- Share from personal experience.
- Own what you are sharing. Use "I" and not "one" or "people often … "
- Give advice only when directly asked for it.
- Allow silence when it occurs naturally.
- Whenever possible, speak from the heart.[8]

Remen writes, "Often when we are listening to another person talk, we are simultaneously thinking about the next thing we are going to say; or running through a critique in our mind about whether we agree with them or not; or considering how we want to respond; or thinking of a story that we want to tell to follow-up (or one-up) the person who is speaking."[7] With this sort of self-dialogue and distraction, it is difficult to hear and understand the meaning and importance of what is being said or empathize with the person who is speaking. The "generous" in *generous listening* refers to an intentional effort to abandon all other agendas and simply listen to know what is important for another person, that is, what matters to him or her. To honor and respect the other person through the act of listening and being fully present.

~◎~

Generous listening means listening without deciding whether you agree or disagree with what is being said or whether you like or dislike what is being said. It means listening without comparing the speaker to yourself: Is he or she more or less highly trained, smarter, more or less competent than I am? It means listening without trying to "fix" the person speaking or to offer advice. It even means listening without trying to understand why the speaker thinks or feels the way that he or she does. Generous listening is listening simply to know what is genuine for another person at the time he or she is speaking. When we listen this way, we offer a place of refuge and safety that allows connection and the open sharing and transformation of ideas.

Adapted from Rachel Naomi Remen, Healer's Art Resource Guide

Confidentiality

Confidentiality is a central tenet in mentoring groups. This is particularly true as the group grows in trust and depth in dialogue. Discussing matters of the self—ones that are perhaps intimate, personal, or cherished—requires a degree of vulnerability among members.

Group members should establish agreements around confidentiality at the onset of the formation of the group. There is not a single right way to come to an agreement about confidentiality; each group should set its own terms. Some may choose to share what they and others say only in general terms with people outside the group without any details or names of specific people or events.

This allows participants to take what they learn to the world outside without betraying sensitive topics. Another group may decide that personal experiences can be discussed outside the group but what others say in the group stays in the group. In essence, participants can discuss what they themselves say or do but agree to not discuss what others say or do. Some groups may decide that all matters discussed in the group should remain confidential and not be discussed outside the group at all. This may be an agreement that applies to all meetings or only particular sessions. A group member may, during the course of a discussion, say, "I would like to ensure that today's discussion remain completely confidential and not be alluded to at all." Whatever the terms, a clear confidentiality agreement allows members to say, "I am willing to be open and honest with you and the risks are worth taking."

In an FMC, honesty, trust, and accountability are fostered by having safeguards around confidentiality. Confidentiality holds participants to the value of treating other persons always as ends in themselves and never as means to another end. We cannot see one another as stepping-stones. FMC group participants should agree that information learned in the context of participation in the group will be held in confidence and will never be used, for example, in order to gain advantage over another person. Maintaining confidentiality shows respect for oneself and others.

At their discretion, there may be times when group members permit one another to go outside the circle and speak about matters to another person—"Please ask professor so-and-so what he thinks of my situation the next time you see him," for example. But barring such special and specific permission, it is imperative for all group members to assume confidentiality as the default position.

In Conclusion

While we have explored various obstacles to forming an FMC and have discussed some ways to jump-start the process, the message here is the pure simplicity of forming an FMC. In this chapter, we have discussed several aspects of what is needed—confidentiality, attendance, participation, and so forth. However, to put this in perspective, it is important as well to highlight what is not needed:

- FMCs do not require expertise to convene, facilitate, or sustain. A group does not need special training in group dynamics or leading discussions, just the willingness to try (and perhaps this book to guide you!).
- FMCs do not require institutional permission. You don't need to take this book to the head of your department with the suggestion that he or she arrange such opportunities for the faculty. FMCs operate independent of the institutional framework of their home colleges. Anyone on campus can take this book and create an FMC for themselves and others who wish to join them.
- FMCs do not require money or other institutional resources. There is no cost to running an FMC, except a modest investment of time. All you need is a space for your gatherings, and although we have suggestions for the kinds of places that we think work the best, none of them necessarily entails a specific cost.

One of the best features of FMCs is that they are disarmingly simple. By adapting the basic guidelines in this book, we believe that even without prior experience, any motivated faculty or staff member is capable of convening and facilitating one.

The first time doing anything typically feels at least a little unsettling. Many of us remember the first class we taught or our first presentation at a professional conference. Even if we now look back fondly at that moment, we can recognize that those were tentative steps. Only later did we hit our stride, becoming comfortable and perhaps even feeling at home with our students and colleagues.

Your initial efforts to create or join an FMC might be cautious or uncertain. Ours were. We hope our stories and advice in this chapter show you what is possible if you are willing to take that first step.

CHAPTER 4

Collaborative Stewardship

Facilitating a Formation Mentoring Community

In chapter 3, we outlined the basic steps for creating a formation mentoring community (FMC) and the factors important for creating a space or container to hold the kind of honest conversations and mentoring that is the essence of an FMC. In this chapter, we move on to discuss the stewardship of an FMC. While many of you no doubt have expertise in teaching a class, leading a discussion, or running a meeting, an FMC calls on a rather unusual model of facilitation. The emphasis is on shared facilitation and creating a level playing field where each member is equally engaged and responsible for the conversation and mentoring that takes place.

Here we describe how shared facilitation works in an FMC, provide suggestions on how to create a level playing field, and discuss how to maintain the integrity of an FMC over time. And then we share some of the ways we've found to get the conversation rolling—resources and ideas for how to open and generate conversation in your FMC.

Facilitating an FMC

The initial convener or facilitator of the group may take the lead in establishing the habits of opening and closing the meeting. But over time, the role is diminished or relinquished as it is shared among the group members. The facilitator does not necessarily need extensive experience in group process, but it is important to remember that this is not a class, so habits of teaching and curriculum design do not necessarily apply and should be put aside. For instance, the facilitator's role is not to direct but to be part of the conversation.

When the convener invites members to join a group, she in essence sets the agenda for the first meeting by providing some framework for why the group is meeting. Framing a thoughtful opening question or beginning with a poignant story can serve as an introduction to the group and model tenets that ultimately are the foundation of formation mentoring groups. Here are some sample openings that we have used, which you also might consider:

- Introduce yourselves to each other by saying why you said yes to the invitation to join the FMC. Perhaps share how you know each other and your hopes and desires for the group.
- Share what inspired you to take up your profession.
- Share something about what each of you is doing that has the greatest meaning for you right now.

During the initial meeting, the group can agree to a set of practices that will shape future conversations. For example, the group may begin each session by having all members check in individually and give brief comments on how they are doing, perhaps mentioning what significant events or insights they have had since the last meeting. This allows every member some time to reflect on the past few weeks and gives each person a voice and a way to contribute to the group conversation. This also allows the distinction between a regular meeting that begins with an agenda or specific action items. Members of the group may decide not to participate in this sharing but should not be deliberately bypassed in the emergent conversation. Beginning with a round of check-ins may be one of many practices that establish some norms for how the group will speak and listen. The way the group talks about these emerging practices will help set the tone for future conversations.

It can be helpful for the facilitator to have something to bring to the table to stimulate the conversation in case nothing else is brought forward from the group. Reflective questions, quotes, wisdom stories, poetry, suggested topics or themes, and meaningful practices may enrich the dialogue and act as points of entry for discussion. She might want to send out the topic by e-mail ahead of time so the members can think about it in advance. But it is of course possible to bring up something spontaneously; in fact, this should be encouraged. It is important to be ready to let go of a previously chosen topic if a more pressing or captivating issue opens up.

The facilitator's role is ideally fleeting. The task is to develop processes that will sustain the group and help it stay true to its common purpose. All groups take on a personality of their own; they evolve and may take on new iterations with subsequent meetings as the members grow together. Indeed, part of the gratification that emerges from the group may come from the manner in which it forms and grows naturally.

Shared Facilitation

Some groups have a convener for the first gathering and then quickly move into shared facilitation where everyone takes a turn. Other groups want a convener to stay in the lead longer before moving to a more democratic way of working. It is worth noting that the equality of the group levels out even further once everyone has been in the facilitator or convener role once.

How do groups share this responsibility? Delegating people to bring something new to talk about each time can help speed up this process. And while the convener may offer structure at the initial gatherings of the FMC, often other processes will emerge spontaneously from other group members. The unfolding of such practices may lead to outcomes both surprising and more profound than the original group agenda.

~☙~ *From Our FMCs*

Taking Turns

During a meeting, a member brought in a very interesting essay as a starting point for a conversation. The discussion was very fruitful. We knew that getting everyone to read an article beforehand, outside of the meeting time, might not always be feasible. He suggested, and we all agreed, that each time a different member would take responsibility to find a piece of writing that spoke to him or her: a professional article, short story, poem, or something else. The member would share the reading with the others ahead of time. But regardless of whether everyone had time to read it ahead of time, the lead person would be prepared to share some thoughts about what he or she had read, introduce a theme to get the conversation going, and help things move along if the conversation stalled. We found that having one person who was accountable for initiating a conversation from something that struck them was great for getting the conversation flowing, though we also agreed that if someone had a burning question or issue that they wanted to bring forward, the prepared piece could be set aside or postponed for the following meeting.

Creating a Level Playing Field

Creating groups of equal participants on a college campus is a special challenge. There are obvious and well-known structures in higher education: rank and tenure, nontenured faculty, administrators, professional staff, and others. Academics are used to being situated squarely within hierarchical and (at least apparently) orderly arrangements. We know our place in the pecking order, know who we report to, who they report to, how money and other resources flow within the institution, who moves the levers of power, and so on. We also know the pathways to power. Much of traditional mentoring on campuses is about guiding younger colleagues along this path. There is both a frustration and comfort in knowing how things work. Clarity and transparency are important, but they also mean that our relationships are often defined by this hierarchical structure. Dislodging us from this arrangement, where we know our place in relation to the others, may not be easy and may require some intentional and thoughtful effort.

Regardless of their positions outside the meetings, all participants in an FMC strive to operate in the group context on a level playing field. Everyone contributes: the eldest, the youngest, the most experienced, the least experienced. Each person's contribution is grist for the mill. Since it tends to cut against the grain, this feature may need to be made explicit from the outset. Everyone comes to be mentored, just as everyone comes to mentor the others. All contributions have equal weight, because all members have valuable perspectives and are asked to speak the truth honestly, as they perceive it.

A key way to level the playing field is for the group convener to bring his or her own problems or questions to the table and ask the other members of the group for their mentoring help. Whether in the process of facilitating the group or after relinquishing this role, it is important that the convener demonstrate a level of vulnerability and trust in the group and participate equally in the conversation.

◦◦◦ *From Our FMCs*

Listening for Clarity

On a very personal level, my FMC has helped me listen better because I am so interested in what my colleagues think and I really value their opinions and thoughts. The other thing that I've been pushed to do is to think more deeply about what I do and how I want to change or refine my professional relationships, mentoring, teaching, etc. Sitting down with colleagues who are different from you but share the same passions and desire to discuss certain nondisciplinary topics is immensely rewarding and thought provoking. It not only changes you, but it changes your relationships and teaching for the better as well.

Some individuals may not be comfortable joining a group that includes members with very different levels of real or perceived power on campus, while others might hesitate to participate in a group of people of the same status due to competition among peers. You cannot eliminate external hierarchies within the FMC, but you (and everyone in the group) can agree to norms for mitigating power and for making the group a place for peer conversation.

Before we set out to form our four groups at Washington, Irvine, Elon, and Gallaudet, we made some conscious decisions regarding the issues of power and the potential pitfalls associated with this. We considered, for example, whether such mentoring groups could be formed with a mix of undergraduate students, faculty, and staff, particularly given that group members need to see and understand one another as peers. After some discussion, we decided that with such a mix, the potential for boundary problems and power differentials was simply too acute. A group of graduate students mixed with faculty and staff seemed to pose fewer problems, though careful attention to the power dynamics would be necessary there as well.

When you start an FMC, consider these realities so that as much as possible, a democratic leveling can take place within the group. This is one of the central aims of an FMC: to create a new, different sort of space, among colleagues on campus, where the usual ways of operating do not apply.

It also needs to be emphasized here that participation in an FMC should not be required or mandated by an institution, a supervisor, or a superior in a workplace setting. Neither should it be made a condition of employment or criteria for advancement. If all members of the group do not enter the process with complete freedom and full responsibility, then accountability and trust will be impossible and the group will not function as it is meant to. Participation must rest on the foundation of the free and responsible initiative of each group member.

While an FMC may indirectly benefit the institution in which it is embedded (it likely will enhance and improve the department or the university as a whole), it primarily exists to create a community in which members strengthen the guiding values that shape their lives and their practice.

~◐◞ *From Our FMCs*

Creating a Level Playing Field

When I convened the Irvine group, the four members were on a level playing field in terms of our academic roles. But there were still some subtle differences in our titles and job descriptions that could have set us moving in the wrong direction if we did

---

not proceed thoughtfully. I convened the group and I was also the director of residency training in the department, so all the members reported to me in some way. I needed to make it clear that I was not leading the group or "chairing the meeting" but was looking to be mentored as much as I was mentoring.

I tried to convey this by explicitly saying this in the first meeting and then by bringing questions and challenges to the table that I had been struggling with and asking them to listen, comment, and advise. I tried to solicit not just feedback on an idea, as I might do at our residency training committee meetings, but actually solicit a different sort of personal mentoring. My experience was that this approach worked well and helped dislodge us from our typical and comfortable roles and relationships.

There were other things, however, that I did not do that probably would have helped in leveling the playing field. Initially I paid little attention to the ways in which the meeting location could change the nature and tone of the meetings. Instead, I went with what was most convenient, which happened to mean meeting in my office. We all worked in the same building and were sometimes rushing to make our meetings on time and then leaving immediately afterward to make it to our clinic or that 1:00 meeting or lecture. So if we had only an hour to meet, then meeting in the building in which all of us worked seemed logical. Meeting rooms were scarce and sometimes tricky to reserve at regular times, and may also have contributed to the sense that we were another planning committee. My office, or so I thought, was a more informal setting where we could be relaxed and communicate freely.

But I did not think very deeply about the fact that it was still *my* office, and I was sitting in my chair, whereas the others were sitting in chairs typically occupied by my patients. In retrospect, this was probably not the best way to dislodge us from our typical roles in the hierarchical ladder or create a more egalitarian space where each member of the group was on a level playing field. It did not occur to me until we, the book authors, met to discuss our groups. When I heard that other groups were meeting off campus, at restaurants, or even at museums, I realized that my choice of meeting space was probably ill advised and may have hindered the aim of an open democratic space for the FMC.

The Opening Session

The opening session is important in helping to form the community and introduce the processes for conversation. The practices and processes that are presented and decided on collectively in the initial sessions form a sort of alchemical container that makes formation and transformation possible. Each of these practices should be agreed on by each member of the group or altered through negotiation so group agreement can be reached.

Besides framing the initial meeting with a question or introductory prompt, the convener should guide the discussion, clarifying what members believe is the purpose of the group, why you are gathering together, what you hope to create, and what constitutes an appropriate space for continued conversation. It is essential that the group as a whole affirm this common purpose.

~ɘɘ *From Our FMCs*

What an FMC Is Not

In our first group meeting, we tried to clarify not only what we hoped the group would become but also what we hoped the group would not become. None of us was really looking for another gripe session, a place to rehearse the familiar complaints about the university, the administration, the department, and so on. We agreed that the group should not be an incubator for bitterness, resentment, or anger. We also agreed that this group would not become another place in which to solve problems or devise programs directly related to our common work of residency training and medical student teaching. Finally, given especially that all of us are professional psychotherapists, we decided that this would not be a group therapy session aimed at dealing with our personal problems or individual neuroses (at least not directly). We would avoid the impulse to fall into a therapeutic stance toward the other group participants.

The members of our budding community appreciated this clarification of boundaries and aims; it was helpful to orient everyone. It also gave us a welcome sense that this was going to be different from what we were used to. It was then fairly clear what the group was not supposed to become. What the group was supposed to become was, and perhaps still is, something of an open question. The answer, while elusive and difficult to define, has become clearer in the course of our shared experience in the FMC.

There are many ways to go about establishing these agreements. Here is a sample of the kinds of questions you might use to help the group think through its purpose and then go on to create its own guidelines and principles:

Willingness
- Are we willing to engage and share with the members in this group?
- Are we willing to help create a container of mutual respect and trust?
- Will I attempt to share my thoughts, feelings, and aspirations?

Respect
- How can we come to know one another?
- How can we honor each other's intentions?
- Can we accept our differences and appreciate them?

Trust
- How do we establish trust in one another?
- Can we follow through with the norms we have agreed on together?
- Are we willing to be open with one another and demonstrate the strength, character, and ability to gain and maintain each other's confidence?

✺ *From Our FMCs*

A First Meeting

To facilitate the initial meeting, I e-mailed my colleagues several days before our first gathering:

In preparation, would you please spend a few minutes writing about why you said "yes" to the invitation to join this project? That writing might serve as a useful introduction to each other

---

105

and to the group. I don't have expectations of what your writing will look like. The format, formality, etc., are up in the air. Since we have at least one visual artist in the group, I'm not certain I should even ask for "writing." Perhaps a better way to put this is to request that you bring something that captures why you said "yes" to our group and what you hope for the group.

This prompt served as a wonderful catalyst in our first meeting. Although some group members had met only in passing before, first-date jitters were fleeting. Each of us had a chance to think in advance about how we wanted to introduce ourselves, and each of us had the opportunity to present more than just our name and department introduction. People actually spoke, uninterrupted, for a couple of minutes, telling something about what motivates and inspires them. One person played a Joan Armatrading song. Within moments of saying hello, we saw many connections between individuals and across the group. We left that discussion yearning for more.

Tending the Container

The convener or facilitator may need to check the container (i.e., the agreed-on norms) at regular intervals to examine its integrity. Are there small chips or cracks developing in the group's container? For example, is one group member habitually tardy? Did another group member in the last meeting interrupt someone or dominate the conversation? When such routine lapses occur, they need to be addressed. If, however, this was an uncharacteristic slip, then it can be forgotten or let go of.

If the convener notices a repeated or chronic problem—a crack in the container—it will require tact, prudence, and discernment to

skillfully address it without further damaging the container itself—
without, for example, alienating the individual who needs to be
reminded of the group agreements. Does prudence suggest that the
convener address the issue in the context of the group as a whole,
using someone's habitual tardiness as a theme for group dialogue?
Or is this problem best addressed by the convener, quietly taking a
person aside one-on-one and making a tactful comment about this
issue?

Rachel Remen suggests that the convener use the group agreements to keep the group members close to their agreements with
each other.[1] When a practice is breached, usually in the thick of
discussion, the convener can simply intervene with a pre-agreed-on
gesture or remind the group with a neutral statement such as, "We
agreed on *no complaining*," to recall the group back to the covenant
between members. These practices ultimately function as the safety
net for the group.

The very manner of maintaining the container may itself be
part of the container—part of the ground rules or norms that govern
the group. A member will not be surprised, or may be less defen-
sive, discussing her tardiness if there was a previous discussion in the
group about the importance of punctuality and that the convener is
responsible for addressing this. If all participants freely agree to such
practices from the start, then it may be easier to interpret the convener's actions as what they are: holding the container in trust rather
than, say, exercising a power play or an attempt to control group
members. Participants will not only expect this from the convener
and, it is hoped, from all members of the group; they will encourage
it when it is not happening.

From time to time, a group may drift away from its core
purpose. It is helpful to have mechanisms in place to periodically
evaluate the FMC itself, to step back and ask:

- To what extent are we staying on track with our original aspirations?
- Are we drifting in the direction of mere pragmatics such as problem solving or work-related planning?
- If so, what do we need to do to get back on track?

The Life Cycles of FMCs

Unlike committees with a specific charge, there is not a designated end point to an FMC. We all have been engaged in our own FMCs for over two years now and cannot anticipate how or when they will end. But we have come to recognize the rhythms that have evolved. This is not to say that all FMCs will follow the same patterns, but considering these cycles and rhythms may be useful to readers.

Breaks and milestones in the academic calendar can provide natural opportunities to reorient the group or revisit and remind the group of the elements in the FMC container. In an academic year, there will be times when not everyone is available to meet. These can be seen as part of a natural cycle for the group. You might want to frame vacations and breaks in the semester as times of reflection. There also can be larger ways of marking the exit and reentry to the FMCs before and after academic breaks. It may be helpful to think of these as a time of integration and a way to have a check-in on the well-being of the group. It can also be an opportunity for an assessment of the growth of the individuals and the group.

It can be helpful to have processes to help the group work through various transitions or as a way to reflect on the growth over the year.

◦◦ *From Our FMCs*

Seasonal Readings FMCs

The Gallaudet group has found two different rhythms that have influenced its discussions: the academic calendar and the seasons of the year. At each meeting at the beginning of the semester, we look forward to that discrete period of time and discuss our wishes. What would we like to see happen in our teaching, our scholarship, and ourselves? These discussions are not simply strategic. They are integrative and help us understand how we can move forward in our thinking, deepen our reflections, and help ourselves to grow. By stating these wishes at the outset of each semester, we break down the intimidating scale of time to smaller units where change can occur. During the course of the semester, members often check in on others' aspirations for change. At the final session of the semester, we reflect back on what happened, what surprised us, what we learned, how we grew, and how we did not.

We also pay close attention to the seasons, marking each new season with a reading from Parker J. Palmer's essays, "Seasons: A Center for Renewal," and then a discussion unfolds about the external seasons and the seasons within us.[2] At the time of this writing, we have made it through a full cycle. It remains to be seen whether this exercise will continue to be fruitful a second and third year. We anticipate that it will, only in different ways.

Recently we also used the readings found in Angeles Arrien's *Living in Gratitude*, which is organized according to the months of the year.[3] On the first day of April, we had read that chapter and spent the ninety-minute session discussing the nature of grace in our lives and the complicated relationship of pride and grace.

When a Member Leaves an FMC

Group members may need opportunities in which they can make a gracious exit from the group as their professional or personal circumstances change over time. Allowing for exit will help group members not feel excessively bound to the group when they no longer are able or willing to participate. When there are breaks (seasons, school year, graduation), we should allow people to graciously leave, close naturally, and also work this in as part of the continuation and renewal of the FMC.

Angeles Arrien encourages groups to make what she calls "honorable closure" by extending appreciation for what the person has contributed. Adapted from her book *The Second Half of Life*, she offers the following conversation questions to help with this process:

- How have I changed?
- How have I grown?
- What new insights and discoveries have I gleaned?
- What is the work I have done, the work I have not done, and the work that I need to do?[4]

Changing the Size and Makeup of an FMC

In addition to the possible flux in membership of an FMC, there may be times when the group will consider changing the size or makeup of the group. Given the democratic nature of FMCs, the entire group should be involved in the discussion of any fundamental changes to the size and makeup of the group. To do this, you would want to consider some questions:

- How do we ensure that the new people will fit in and feel welcomed by the group?

- How will the new members change the nature of the group and its dynamics?

Inviting a New Member

When a new member comes in, you can view this as an opportunity for reformulating your group. Prior to the person joining the group, you or other members of your FMC might want to meet with him or her to convey the group process, where the group has been, and the themes discussed.

The first meeting with the new member is a good time to review all the agreements. The principles and purpose should be restated to orient the new member, help the original members recall them, and reestablish the collective agreement for the new whole.

∼✦∽ *From Our FMCs*

Inviting in Someone New

We wondered how we could invite someone into our space: the container of our group was already deeply formed. But we also knew that it was important to bring in some new energy to the group. We decided it would be best to invite two people at a time, so that the balance of having two new members would counter the weight of the three already together and be more welcoming to the new members. In this act, the three sustaining members became the conveners, not a single individual summoning others to the group, but three already engaged in formation work, wanting to deepen the work by extending the invitation to others.

Priming the Pump: Openings and Closings

There are multiple ways to effectively open and close each FMC gathering. Repeated practices and routines can help establish the atmosphere and context for the group. This could be as simple as taking a moment of silence before everyone begins to allow people a chance to settle in. The key point is to create a moment in time to draw everyone into the group so they are fully present. There are many examples of these kinds of practices. Rather than repeat them all here, we refer to several excellent books in the "Convening and Facilitation" section of the Recommended Resources section at the back of the book.

The Gallaudet group has used a variety of methods to get started. For some meetings, nothing has been planned, which has worked some times better than others. They have often had each member bring in a short poem. One particularly fruitful poem early on was "The Way It Is," by William Stafford, which was helpful in their discussions. On another occasion, one of the members created a single piece of paper with five quotes on the topic of intention, a concept that the member had wanted to discuss. They have posted this well-designed paper in their offices. As a result of this idea, the Gallaudet group is beginning to bring a single sheet of paper to prompt discussions around a particular topic.

At the University of Washington group, members always start with a formal round of checking in. There is no formal closure, but they do acknowledge one another and sum up what has transpired during the meeting. For the first year or so, the University of California Irvine group used a round of checking in prompted by the simple question, "Where are you?" This was typically sufficient to carry the conversation through the entire meeting. Group members eventually brought questions to the group that they sought counsel or mentoring on. Closure typically involves a brief discussion of a theme that they want to continue or start conversing about in the next gathering.

The Elon group has a circumscribed period of informal chitchat at the restaurant, which ends after they order food. They end the meeting by identifying a topic or question that they want to address the next time. One of the group members likes to write as they talk, so she makes notes on the discussion and recaps the points at the end. They intentionally make a point of saying good-bye to one another rather than just scattering, as often happens at the close of lunch meetings.

୰ଡ଼୰ *From Our FMCs*

Reflective Writing Exercise

Before a break in the semester, the Elon group decided to try a writing exercise that this book's authors had been introduced to by Megan Scribner, a professional editor. Here is the e-mailed description of the process.

୰ଡ଼୰

Before we meet next, each of us should find a time when we can write for twenty or thirty minutes, uninterrupted. Get comfortable. Think about a topic that we've discussed over the past year, or one that we should have discussed [smile].

Start writing. Don't edit or polish, just write. You might tell a story, unpack an idea, mess around with something complicated, raise questions that aren't (or can't be) resolved, or . . . This isn't meant to be high academic prose, although it can be if that's what floats your boat. When you're finished writing (and, really, don't write for hours; just do a focused burst), hit Print, and bring copies to pass around.

When we meet, each of us will read her or his writing to the group. After a person reads her or his piece, each of us will write

---

for five or so minutes, riffing on what we heard. These riffs are not editorial; they are not critiques. They are your free responses to something that resonated for you, such as: "What you wrote reminded me of this story, made me think about this question . . ." Then we read the riffs and have a brief discussion of what the original writing sparked. Then we move to the next person. Rinse, repeat.

Does that make sense? If you have questions or concerns, please raise them with the whole group or just with me. The first time I did this, it was not entirely comfortable for me: I tend to outline before I write, I tend not to write in first person, and so on. But once I stopped stressing about how unusual it was, I found that I enjoyed it a great deal. I wrote with a different voice (actually, different voices in different rounds of writing), and that was both fun and revealing. So, no stress, no competition, no worries about how productive you are (Did I write enough?). Just write for twenty minutes. Then smile and hit Print.

Readings

Some of the most effective FMC meetings are those in which a short passage, a quote, or a poem has been shared with the group. We have found that "homework" usually doesn't work, so it's important that the reading be short, something that can be read in one to three minutes in the group. While a reading might be proposed, something else might come up and the planned theme will need to be shelved for another time. It is important to be flexible. No recipe or formula determines the choice of readings. The loss of a colleague may prompt a poem or reading having to do with loss and healing. The birth of a child may prompt a reading that offers hope and support. Perhaps an inspiring speech or essay provides grist for the conversation mill. There may well be times when a group member's simple observation or insight becomes the point of discussion for the group.

∾ *From Our FMCs*

Prose Can Open the Door

Our group read and discussed a short essay, "Gate 4," by Naomi Shihab Nye.[5] The story is about how the author, while waiting in an airport, heard an announcement: "If anyone in the vicinity of Gate 4-A understands any Arabic, please come to the gate immediately." What ensued was the coming together of strangers, spontaneous acts of kindness, generosity, and community. The essay leaves the reader with a sense that there is hope for our ability to form community across differences and that "not everything is lost."

I asked the group to read the story slowly—with careful attention to language and underlying meaning. Discussing the short essay allowed our group to imagine the kind of community we want to create, envision the kind of space where we can encounter each other in new ways. The essay created an entry into a discussion about ourselves and the place we work, the kind of world we want to live in, how to stay rooted, and the relationships we need the most.

Topics and Themes for Discussion

There are many topics and themes you can use to generate meaningful conversation in your group. Some are briefly discussed and accompanied by reflection questions in chapter 2, though an FMC should not limit itself to these themes. For any topic, you may want to ask questions to help the group begin to consider the personal meaning of the passage. Then suggest that each member take a few minutes to read the selected passage, being sure to give them some additional reflection time to let the piece settle in. You might also suggest that each person take a few minutes to write down his or her reflections. It may take some time for the group to get used to the idea that these writings aren't meant to be critical interpretations of the text but a time to seek the personal import of it. The facilitator may want to share a few reflections of his own, to help model this kind of conversation.

~◎~ *From Our FMCs*

Campus Inspirations

On a spring day I walked into a monthly meeting with a colleague. She asked me if I would mind going on a walk with her. She did not say where we were going. We walked for a few minutes, and when we arrived at a cluster of trees, she asked me to look up. I saw a dozen or more large nests resting at the top of the trees. I was astonished at the size of the nests and the amount of activity and sounds emanating from the nests. My colleague pointed out that we were looking at a heron's rookerie. The eggs had just hatched, thus the noise and activity. I was bewildered by this discovery. How could I have walked by this space for so many years and not noticed? I was all the more humbled by the reality that these herons' nests were an annual ritual for these ancient creatures.

The next week, one by one, I invited members of my FMC to take a walk with me. I asked them to look up and take in the sound and the wonderment of the herons' nests in our midst. I now ask members of the group as they walk the campus, enter classrooms, move through hallways, to try to notice something they had not seen before.

CHAPTER 5

From Individual to Institutional Change

Ripples of Transformation

Formation mentoring communities are about facilitating construc-
tive changes. These changes typically begin with individuals, but
then they ripple out from the group, making what may seem at
first to be only small waves on the surface of a campus. Over time,
however, those ripples have the potential to create institutional and
cultural transformation on campuses and in higher education.

This is not the typical path of reform in the academy. Most efforts
at wide-scale change in higher education follow a conventional path
that Richard L. Morrill calls "strategic leadership."[1] This approach
focuses on patterns of influence and power within organizations.
Although proponents of this vision advocate moving beyond the
traditional concerns with a leader's formal authority or personal
charisma, they emphasize the importance of relational leaders
who are skilled at asking questions, setting agendas, and building
consensus.

Recently some in higher education have raised the possibilities
of "disruptive innovation."[2] This framework for change is inspired

by the ways Web-based technologies have transformed businesses, including music sales, video rentals, and bookstores. In these businesses, outside factors quickly prompt radical revisions by offering fundamental challenges to traditional structures and assumptions. To respond to these disruptions, we are told, colleges and universities must be flexible and cost-conscious, holding on to their essential values but abandoning outdated habits and programs.

While strategic leadership and disruptive innovation will undoubtedly influence the future of higher education, FMCs offer a different path toward transformation. These groups are based on the assumption that lasting change does not always come from the top down or the outside in; sometimes the most meaningful change comes from the bottom up and the inside out. In social movements, like those for racial and gender equality in the United States, activists developed power sources that were not embedded in formal organizational structures. Only after building capacity and momentum among like-minded individuals did they attempt to reform social frameworks. As Parker J. Palmer points out, such movements "abandon the logic of organizations in order to gather the power necessary to rewrite the logic of organizations."[3]

Parker J. Palmer's Stages of Change

1. Isolated individuals decide to stop leading "divided lives."
2. These people discover each other and form groups for mutual support.
3. Empowered by community, they learn to translate "private problems" into public issues.
4. Alternative rewards emerge to sustain the movement's vision, which may force the conventional reward system to change.[4]

We are not so bold as to equate FMCs with the civil rights or women's movements. Indeed, the early signs of institutional change sparked by FMCs are too new to prompt any universal claims. Yet on all four of our campuses, we have witnessed the many small instances of change that naturally emerge when isolated individuals come together in mutual support, and we have observed how these changes begin to ripple out from individual FMCs. To illustrate that process, we offer four brief reflections on what we have experienced.

FMC Ripples at the University of Washington

The ripples of the mentoring community work at the University of Washington have many sources, but common to all are the efforts of courageous, inspired, and capable educators who manage to find one another and engage in questions that matter. One such group of colleagues is involved in the Courage to Teach and Lead movement.[5] The questions underlying the courage movement are but one example of those that can be used in formation work of any kind: How do we go about the work of renewing the heart, mind, spirit, and exploration of the inner landscape of an educator's life? How do we connect and reconnect to the fundamental purpose of our work in a way that has integrity? How do we create safe spaces and trusting relationships in education in the formation of community?

These questions have long deep roots at UW and have been my companions for many years. I was fortunate to have done my doctoral work during a time when some of our faculty published seminal work on these kinds of questions and the moral dimensions of education. Roger Soder, John Goodlad, and others all have ties in some way or another to the big questions that relate to the work of mentoring communities.

119

On numerous occasions, I have been encouraged to wade into this water and join the exploration of these questions. Yet although I have been in the presence of the courage work for many years, somehow I could not find a way to unite this with my own life's work. I imagined that this work was primarily for K–12 teachers, particularly those who need to find ways to renew their commitment to their work. I did not have a vision for how this would apply to postsecondary education, no less at a research university as complex as the one I have taught in for more than fifteen years. Even now, I cannot say that I am fully articulate about the nuanced way that integrative education connects to the aims of liberal education, particularly in the context of a truly diverse and multifaceted university.

Ironically, I most often responded by saying, "It sounds interesting, but I don't really have the time right now." But then I fell into this work with the FMCs and found myself talking about community, the university as a common space, the integration of the self in our work, and dialogue and friendship. On several occasions, my colleagues asked about the nature of these biannual meetings. I found it hard to explain that I am part of a group that is talking about formation of the self and ultimately about transforming higher education. I gave my best answer with the hope of some understanding. Others asked me to describe in brief the main purpose of the book I was writing with my friends and colleagues. They responded with interest, intrigued by what we were about. Given where I live and work, I should not have been surprised to learn that there is a substantial community of educators who in some way would be connected to, invigorated by, and desirous of this work.

I have begun to meet individually with colleagues who want to discuss the possibility of forming a group of like minds from across campus—a group born of the interests of an ethicist, a physician, a doctoral candidate, and a staff member at UW. We are people who have been talking, imagining, and wanting something more. We are people who believe in the work of the university. In fact, we are a collection of people who understand that a research university is precisely the place where the seeds of free speech are sown and the place where we ought to be inspired by ideas, discourse, the intersection of living our lives, and learning as we do so.

With minimal effort, we found each other and found time to be in conversation. We established a loose set of principles creating the time and space to begin a conversation about ourselves and our work. Indeed, what is emerging is another formation mentoring group.

I am now fully immersed in the water, and the ripples are spreading across this campus. I am no longer surprised to encounter others who have decided at some point that it is worth wading in—that it is worth the risk and that these ripples connect us to each other and a long-standing tradition of struggle and exploration in higher education.

FMC Ripples at Elon University

The FMC ripples at Elon are small yet real. For all five members of our FMC, our lunchtime conversations have clarified our values and priorities, leading us to understand and do our work in new ways.

When our FMC first met, we talked a lot about our institution's culture. Although we all appreciated many aspects of Elon, we felt we were swimming against a current of busyness that threatened to wash us out to sea. We wanted to connect more deeply with our students, our teaching, our scholarship, our colleagues, and our lives off-campus, but we seemed to spend most of our time and energy rushing from one thing to the next.

As we talked, we returned repeatedly to the question of what it means to be "productive." Must being productive always mean doing more, always striving for external measures of excellence? Could we possibly broaden the term to include going deeper and doing less better? We resolved as a group, partly in jest, to spend our time together *not* being productive. We would not keep notes on our conversations. We would not develop a research project, a teaching initiative, or a mentoring program. Instead we would be productive by being attentive to each other and the group. That felt distinctly countercultural. And it required us to make choices that went against our prevailing habits—saying no to other seemingly purposeful activities so that we could share Thai food and be unproductive together.

That commitment has sustained us as a group and has rippled out for each of us as individuals. Nina, for example, now thinks differently about how she mentors new faculty in her department. In the past, she would focus her efforts on basic needs, asking, "How are you doing?" and volunteering to help with nuts-and-bolts concerns. She still starts with those sorts of issues, but she then moves gently toward deeper questions, supporting her new colleagues to reflect on what they need to feel professionally fulfilled and meaningfully connected on campus.

As a group, we also have adopted a new way of connecting with our students. While each of us has strong, even inspiring, relationships with some students, we have found that many of our students seemed somewhat afraid of us. Students who are struggling in our courses sometimes approach us cautiously, not wanting to interrupt our more important work and clearly not understanding that *they* are our most important work. One day over curry and noodles, Mary told us of a simple technique she adopted from a retired colleague. Mary requires each of her students to visit her during office hours in the first weeks of the semester. That introductory meeting, Mary said, seemed to break the ice with students, allowing them to talk with her later about their confusion with class material or their other questions about college and life. Now all of us have adopted some version of this approach, and we can see the small but real effects it has had on our students' learning and our relationships with them.

We each have also shared stories of how our FMC conversations have influenced decisions we have made in our professional lives. Samantha, for instance, now approaches her annual performance report differently, writing and talking with her department chair about her intention of living a more balanced life, which means setting goals not only about classes to be taught and art to be created and exhibited, but also about time spent renewing herself and connecting with the natural world, the inspiration for much of her art. Similarly, Darris has decided to focus his Ph.D. research on a topic of personal importance that also has significance in his field rather than the more conventional choice that he had anticipated when he began his doctoral program.

Although none of these ripples have grown into a wave that has washed across the entire university, each one is affecting not only us as individuals but also our relationships with our students and departmental colleagues. And we all smile now when we hear colleagues raise questions about what it means to be a productive member of our busy campus community.

FMC Ripples at Gallaudet University

It did not take long for the Gallaudet FMC to have a ripple effect into the physical and symbolic space of an academic department. In the first semester of our FMC meetings, Robert raised the issue of accountability. This topic emerged out of a discussion of whether faculty in our department (ourselves included) devoted enough time to students and whether that time was of a deeper quality than the business-only interactions so often found in faculty offices. As an example, Robert pointed out that we should look at how the windows in the office doors in our department are covered up with various materials. Originally intended to create a deaf-friendly design that extended the visual reach of both the office denizens and the passersby, Robert noted how every faculty member had fully covered the glass, sending the message to students, "Go away, I'm busy." If we were really open for our students, we would literally and figuratively let them be able to see what is on the inside.

Grudgingly, I noted that he had a point. My window was fully covered in order to increase my privacy and productivity. It did not invite students into my office space. We realized that if we were serious about being accountable and more present with students and colleagues, we needed to embody that change somehow. We decided that we would redesign our office windows. The following day, Melissa created a new cover for her door leaving a window to see through, and I cleared a space for students to see in. Robert had already ensured that the students could see through the window in his door. Through the act of modifying our windows, we symbolically showed our commitment to be open and available to our students and colleagues.

But a symbol is not enough. The quality of the time that is spent within the office space had to change as well. This is particularly important for, as we often discussed during the first year of our FMC, we share a common disciplinary grounding—Deaf Studies—which requires students to reflect on personal issues of identity, power, and oppression. It is not uncommon for students to be unsettled by the challenging social questions they encounter in their course work—questions that have deep personal and existential significance. Prior to our regular FMC meetings, I had a sense of the depth to which students wrestle with the personal nature of the topics raised, yet I did not fully appreciate how being present for students would require more from me as a person.

The ripples of the FMC extend both inward and outward. Prior to joining the original Fetzer Foundation–sponsored project and the subsequent FMCs that formed, I was an unlikely candidate for this sort of work. Not given to habits of reflection and introspection, I moved through the world, face forward, always looking to the next thing, with a frenetic and enthusiastic abandon. From our FMC conversations, though, I have become much more mindful about the need to develop new ways of being with others in the world. These new ways include a different sort of engagement with others that allows me to slow down and to see and listen with a wider set of eyes and ears to not only what is being said directly, but also on the periphery. This internal ripple of the FMC, I have come to see, is essential to the ripples outward. Creating an opening in the office window may seem like a small act with no institutional significance, yet it is symbolic of the essential seed for institutional change—individual change that is sustained by a community of colleagues holding one another accountable to their desires for a better self, better relationships with their students, and a better future for higher education.

FMC Ripples at the University of California Irvine

At a faculty meeting in the Department of Psychiatry, our associate dean for faculty development presented data from our recent faculty survey. The data suggested that most faculty in the School of Medicine were pleased with their own work, but they expressed a pervasive sense of dissatisfaction with the wider institution and the lack of support for their efforts in the institutional culture. Burnout risk was high; retention of junior faculty members was a problem. Only 9 percent of faculty indicated that they had ever received any professional mentoring.

As the meeting continued, Rebecca, a faculty member who would soon be leaving the institution, expressed that the thing she would miss the most after leaving would be her participation in our FMC. As she talked about the FMC and how she had benefited from her participation, the associate dean was intrigued. She was especially pleased and surprised to hear that we included a physician from outside our department in the group. Physicians from psychiatry regularly meeting with a physician from internal medicine to talk about their work? This was a novel concept! She was also intrigued that such a group had been convened and sustained without university resources or a specific institutional mandate. And naturally, she was impressed that this was the one thing that a departing faculty member would miss most after leaving.

As she considered how best to respond to the dissatisfaction expressed in the faculty survey, the associate dean saw great potential in the FMC model of peer mentoring to address the felt needs of faculty and administrators. As individuals, the faculty seemed content, but as colleagues, as part of a larger institutional whole, there was widespread discontentment. Perhaps more FMCs on campus would be an effective way to address many of these problems. We soon arranged to meet and discuss this.

At our subsequent meeting, I explained to her the genesis and the history of the FMC model, going back to the initial gathering of faculty convened by the Fetzer Institute. I recalled how this group of authors chose to convene and study peer mentoring groups on our four campuses, under the guidance of our two senior mentors. I then recounted the experiences of the FMC groups at Irvine, the University of Washington, Elon, and Gallaudet and explained the reasons we decided to write this book. "It's not a top-down model that is mandated from above," I explained. "You don't need money, permission from the department chair, or an institutional mandate to begin an FMC group."

"As I understand it, you selected people to participate and targeted personal invitations to the initial group members," the associate dean said. "How do you respond to the potential objection that these groups are elitist and not for everyone?" I replied that the groups are in fact "populist" and not elitist, because the criteria for selecting people to invite had virtually nothing to do with their CV or their professional accomplishments as these are generally measured. "Academic rank and tenure, or external prestige, did not really factor in." Rather, the criteria had simply to do with "readiness" for something like this. It is true that not everyone would be interested in or open to participating in such a group. And with our initial small group, we did not capture everyone who might want to participate, but we had to begin somewhere. This was a "small is beautiful" model of change that did not need to include everyone right away; if there was more interest, more groups could form.

The associate dean recognized the potential in FMCs to address several of the problems and challenges at our School of Medicine. As her enthusiasm for the idea grew, she asked me, "What would you need to roll this out in the rest of the medical school?" I replied that besides more time, the only thing we really needed from the institution was perhaps some spaces to meet. And if that was not available, we could simply have groups meet off campus.

I also clarified my role: "I am not the faculty mentoring expert, and these are not 'my' groups. People do not need me in order to convene and sustain them. What they need is the kind of encouragement and experience that this book provides and a bit of daring to go out there and try something new." But, I noted, we could use institutional "occasions" to introduce people to the idea of FMCs, so long as no deans or department chairs institutionalized the model by requiring faculty to participate or

127

join a group. The leadership of the university needed to understand that participation had to come solely from an individual's intrinsic desire to join such a group. "It is essential that participation in these groups is not bound up with faculty advancement or other institutional objectives," I explained.

We decided that I would present the concept and the history of FMCs at the dean's leadership council meeting in the spring. We would then arrange to present the model of FMCs at various departmental Grand Rounds lectures the next fall when the new academic year began. If people then came forward and expressed interest, we would encourage them to convene an FMC and provide them with assistance, encouragement, and support. This way of proceeding would maintain the grassroots nature of the groups, while also allowing us to sow the seeds and help more people understand this model. If several groups convened and continued to operate on campus, we could then study outcomes in a year or two, seeing, for example, whether responses on the faculty survey were affected by participation in an FMC.

Although we would be using institutional means to introduce the model of FMCs to campus, we would maintain the essential empowering features of these groups. They would continue to develop from the ground up, not the top down. Once other FMCs took root, careful outcomes research could help us see more clearly how such groups affect individual outcomes for participants and perhaps the culture of the institution as a whole.

In Conclusion

As these examples suggest, even at this early date in the process, the ripples of change that FMCs initiate have the capacity to touch, even to mold, organizational practices and structures across our campuses. Although leadership, technology, and many other factors shape higher education, we believe that personal change always precedes widespread cultural change, and in some cases, it can drive institutional change. Big things most often begin on a small, manageable, and very human scale—as small as four or five people sitting and talking about their hopes and dreams. That's true on our campus and perhaps on yours too.

Although this is not an "academic book," it is a book for academics. We hope it has spoken to your situation, perhaps to your predicament. We also hope our reflections and suggestions have been not just informative but also empowering and that you have been inspired to take up questions of meaning, purpose, and values in your work and bring these into conversations with colleagues.

There is no formula or precise method for creating and sustaining FMCs. We, the authors, all made and learned from mistakes along the way, and each of us brought a unique approach to convening our FMCs. So take the recommendations in this book as simply that: friendly suggestions and helpful ideas to get you moving along in the right direction. Trust that if you take some steps to bring interested people together, good things will happen.

Our parting advice is simple. Run up a flag on your campus and see who else is out there; drop a little stone in the pond and watch the ripples spread. All it takes to launch an FMC is the desire to pursue your work in a deeper way and a willingness to try something different. If our experience is any indication, it won't be long before your colleagues will thank you for it.

AFTERWORD:
BEYOND THE SMALL GROUP

One of the oldest wisdom stories about how change happens, "The Story of the Birthday of the World," is attributed to Rabbi Isaac Luria, a sixteenth-century Kabbalist. Like many other stories about change, it includes a cosmology, a theory about how the world is made. According to this story, our world is not broken; our world is hidden. The rabbi's story goes like this:

In the beginning, there was only the Holy Darkness, the Source of Life. At some unknown time in the history of things, the world as we know it, the world of a "thousand thousand things," emerged as a ray of light from the heart of the Holy Darkness, and when this happened, there was an accident: The vessels that contained the wholeness of the world broke open, and the wholeness of the world scattered into an infinite number of sparks of wholeness that fell into all people and all events and all institutions, where they remain deeply hidden until this very day.

According to the story, the whole human race is a response to this accident. We are here for a purpose: we have been born because we are able to discern the hidden wholeness in all people and all institutions. We can witness the hidden wholeness in each other and remind each other of it. We can support each other in finding the courage to live by it once again, and by doing so, we can heal the world back to its original wholeness. Restoring the world back to its original wholeness is not the work of experts; it is the work of ordinary human beings. People just like us can heal the world, its people, and its institutions with our listening, our belief in each other, and the gift of our friendship and community.

In the more common way of thinking, making institutional change requires individuals to persuade those with power to take a new path or, at a minimum, grant people permission to change. This perceived dependence often frustrates reformers and constrains visions of change to what seems practical, political, or doable within a certain context. But in our personal experience, institutional change often starts differently; it starts among those who experience the problem and feel the need for change the most personally and intimately. The impulse for change grows close to the ground, gaining wisdom and strategy from experience and learning from mistakes, incubating the green shoots of a new way of being and doing. Its methods are usually simple and accessible to all.

Technology can support change, but sustainable change is always rooted in our relationships and our mutual connection to common dreams and values. It is nurtured in community by meeting together to remember what matters and encourage personal change, not in our core values but in our courage to live by them. In such small communities, people find others who are committed to supporting them in living their professional lives differently, and support others as well.

As the people involved begin to experience benefits from this new way of being, they pass on their enthusiasm to others at their institutions. They talk about their experiences at coffee, at dinner parties, at committee meetings. They tell their students and their families. Their professional relationships change in subtle but important ways. They seem happier and more excited about their work, or more creative or more resilient to stress. Others think, "What do they have going for them?" and then, "Why not?" and they too begin to meet and talk, and gradually a groundswell begins within an institution.

As the method of change replicates itself, it adapts and becomes more effective at promoting change in people and the ways they think and do things. After a time, some of the people involved are promoted within their institution and talk to an even wider circle of people. Some of those they speak to are within the institution, and some are not. Others take jobs at different institutions and start the process anew. People write about it in newsletters and professional journals. They talk about it at professional conferences and national meetings. Someone begins a blog. Someone else writes a book. Even more people say, "Why not?" and gradually over time, a movement is born.

Throughout history, human beings have always connected and generated change through meaningful conversations that began small and sometimes ended up as a transformative movement within an institution or society. In a simple and organic way, conversations that remind people of what is important and help them to integrate it more closely into their daily lives can eventually restore our institutions and even our world back into its original wholeness.

The six doctors who met in Rachel's living room seventeen years ago did not plan to start a movement. They gathered because all of them felt a loss of meaning and passion in their work and had begun to think about doing something different. They had each come to medicine because of core values that went back to childhood and because somewhere along the way, each came to believe that medicine offered a chance to live by these values. But after years of doctoring within medical institutions, this had not proven to be the case.

They decided to meet once a month in the evening and organized the conversation around a few simple interactional guidelines that made everyone feel safe: confidentiality, honesty, generous listening, respect for diversity. No interruptions. No unsolicited advice. For the first six months, they simply listened to one another uncover core values they all held in common and in secret. Most of them had never shared these thoughts with another doctor before. They began to tell each other stories and share diverse experiences from their work as physicians that embodied the common values and qualities of their medical lineage. It did not matter that they were surgeons, pediatricians, obstetricians, cardiologists, and psychiatrists. In these meetings, they were all simply doctors. Each time they met, they chose as a focus for the evening's stories a quality, value, or experience that was an innate part of their daily work: healing, altruism, service, kindness, listening, loss, pain, judgment, harmlessness, refuge, reverence for life. They shared poems and writings from world literature about the evening's topic. They shared their own poems and writings as well. After a while, someone suggested naming the group "Finding Meaning in Medicine."

Gradually these doctors talked to others who asked to join the conversation. When the group became too large for everyone to share their stories and thoughts during a single meeting, some doctors took the initiative and started new conversation groups among their own doctor friends or at their own workplaces. More groups formed. More doctors had the opportunity to talk about their group experience at their workplaces and elsewhere. Eventually doctors talked about the personal benefits of their group experiences at local and national medical meetings, or they wrote about it in medical journals. And still more groups formed. Ten years ago a very short *Finding Meaning Group Resource Guide* was written that described the simple method and its outcomes, and it was passed from hand to hand. Five or six years ago, it was posted on a website so that anyone in the world can download it and establish their own Finding Meaning group.[1]

Seventeen years is a long time. There are now hundreds of Finding Meaning in Medicine storytelling groups in hospitals and in living rooms across the country and in more than half of America's medical schools. There are groups in twelve other countries. There are Finding Meaning in Medicine groups, Finding Meaning in Nursing groups, and Finding Meaning in Veterinary Medicine groups. There are Finding Meaning in Service groups for psychologists, chaplains, and social workers, and Finding Meaning in Medical School groups for medical students. For a while, there was even a group of mothers in the Midwest that called itself Finding Meaning in Motherhood. Perhaps starting a movement is as simple as finding a living room, three or four interested friends who share a common calling, and the time to reflect on what really matters and listen deeply to one another.

Rabbi Luria suggests that change starts with helping each other remember ourselves. The poet Mark Nepo has said that each of us has at our core an unencumbered "spot of grace," a set of values, perspectives, and actions which encompass our essential identity. "To know this spot of inwardness is to know who we are," he tells us, and this is a "hard life-long task, for the nature of becoming is a constant filming over of where we begin while the nature of being is a constant erosion of what is not essential. We each live in the midst of this ongoing tension, growing tarnished or covered over only to be worn back to that incorruptible spot of grace at our core."[2]

To live as who we are and by what we believe is a human need. When we deliberately engage each other in the process of self-remembering and befriend in one another the courage to act from our essential values, we may be able to uncover all that has become tarnished in our institutions and make real a better world.

Rachel Naomi Remen
Angeles Arrien

RECOMMENDED RESOURCES

For thousands of years, people have studied how human interactions lead to meaningful growth and connection. From that rich lineage, we gathered this very brief overview for readers who want to go deeper into the roots of this book and this work. This section highlights some of the most helpful resources on education, convening and facilitating groups, dialogue and conversations, formation and spiritual direction, mentoring, and community.

We hope that these references will support you in your own transformative adventure and your formation mentoring communities.

Education

Antonio, A. L., M. J. Chang, K. Hakuta, D. A. Kenny, S. L. Levin, and J. F. Milem. "Effects of Racial Diversity on Complex Thinking in College Students." *Psychological Science* 15 (2004): 507–510.

Astin, Alexander W., Helen S. Astin, and Jennifer A. Lindholm. *Cultivating the Spirit: How College Can Enhance Students' Inner Lives.* San Francisco: Jossey-Bass, 2007.

Chapman-Walsh, Diane. *Trustworthy Leadership: Can We Be the Leaders We Need Our Students to Become?* Kalamazoo, MI: Fetzer Institute, 2006.

Charon, Rita. *Narrative Medicine: Honoring the Stories of Illness.* New York: Oxford University Press, 2006.

Christensen, Clayton M., and Henry J. Eyring. *The Innovative University: Changing the DNA of Higher Education from the Inside Out.* San Francisco: Jossey-Bass, 2011.

Goleman, Daniel. *Emotional Intelligence: Why It Can Matter More Than IQ.* New York: Bantam Books, 1995.

Goodlad, John I., Roger Soder, and Kenneth A. Srotnik, eds. *The Moral Dimensions of Teaching.* San Francisco: Jossey-Bass, 1990.

Inchausti, Robert. *SpitWad Sutras: Classroom Teaching as Sublime Vocation.* New York: Bergin and Garvey, 1993.

Morrill, Richard L. *Strategic Leadership: Integrating Strategy and Leadership in Colleges and Universities.* Lanham, MD: Rowan & Littlefield, 2010.

O'Donnell, J. F., M. R. Rabow, and R. N. Remen. "The Healer's Art: Awakening the Heart of Medicine." *Medical Encounter-Medical Encounter* 1 (2007): 7–11.

Palmer, Parker J. *The Courage to Teach: Exploring the Inner Landscape of a Teacher's Life* (10th anniversary ed.). San Francisco: Jossey-Bass, 2007.

Palmer, Parker J. *Healing the Heart of Democracy: The Courage to Create a Politics Worthy of the Human Spirit.* San Francisco: Jossey-Bass, 2011.

Palmer, Parker J, and Arthur Zajonc. *The Heart of Higher Education: A Call to Renewal.* San Francisco: Jossey-Bass, 2010.

Parks, Sharon. *The Critical Years: Young Adults and the Search for Meaning, Faith and Community.* San Francisco: HarperCollins, 1991.

Pink, Daniel. *A Whole New Mind: Why Right Brainers Will Rule the Future.* New York: Penguin, 2006.

Rabow, M., J. Wrubel, and R. Remen. "The Promise of Professionalism: Mission Statements Among a National Cohort of Healer's Art Medical Students." *Annals of Family MedicineAnnals of Family Medicine* 7 (2009): 336–342.

Rabow, M. W., M. Newman, and R. N. Remen. "What Faculty Learn: The Impact on Faculty Facilitators of Teaching 'The Healer's Art.'" *Teaching and Learning in Medicine* (forthcoming). http://www.ishiprograms.org/findingmeaning.

Remen, Rachel Naomi. *Finding Meaning in Medicine Resource Guide*. Bolinas, CA: Institute for the Study of Health and Illness Press, 2002. http://www.ishiprograms.org/finding meaning.

Remen, R. N., J. O'Donnell, and M. W. Rabow. "The Healer's Art: Education in Meaning and Service." *Journal of Cancer EducationJournal of Cancer Education* 23 (2008): 65–67.

Remen, R., and M. Rabow. "The Healer's Art: Professionalism, Service and Mission." *Medical EducationMedical Education* 39 (2005): 1167–1168.

Schumacher, E. F. *A Guide for the Perplexed*. New York: Harper Perennial, 1980.

Schumacher, E.F. *Small Is Beautiful*: *Economics as If People Mattered*. New York: Harper Perennial, 1989.

Senge, Peter. *Presence: Human Purpose and the Field of the Future*. New York: Doubleday, 2004.

Soder, Roger. *The Language of Leadership*. San Francisco: Jossey-Bass, 2001.

Convening and Facilitation

Art of Hosting: "A Four-Fold Way of Hosting." 2010. http://www.artofhosting.org/theart/a4-foldway

Baldwin, Christina, and Ann Linnea. *The Circle Way: A Leader in Every Chair*. San Francisco: Berrett-Koehler, 2011.

Garfield, C. A., C. Spring, and S. Cahill. *Wisdom Circles: A Guide to Self-Discovery and Community Building in Small Groups*. New York: Hyperion Books, 1998

Jacobson, Micah, and Mari Ruddy. *Open to Outcome: A Practical Guide for Facilitating and Teaching Experiential Reflection*. Bethany, OK: Wood 'N' Barnes Publishing, 2004.

Miller, Dan, Buzz Bocher, and Steven Simpson. *The Processing Pinnacle: An Educator's Guide to Better Processing*. Bethany, OK: Wood 'N' Barnes Publishing, 2006.

Neal, Craig, and Patricia Neal. *The Art of Convening: Authentic Engagement in Meetings, Gatherings, and Conversations*. San Francisco: Berrett-Koehler, 2011.

Schuman, Sandy, ed. *Creating a Culture of Collaboration: The International Association of Facilitators Handbook*. San Francisco: Jossey-Bass, 2006.

Stanchfield, Jennifer. *Tips and Tools: The Art of Experiential Group Facilitation*. Bethany, OK: Wood 'N' Barnes Publishing, 2008.

Dialogue and Conversation

Bohm, David. *On Dialogue*. New York: Routledge, 1996.

Brown, Juanita, and David Isaacs. *The World Café: Shaping Our Futures Through Conversations That Matter*. San Francisco: Berrett-Koehler, 2005. http://www.theworld cafecommunity.org/

Ellinor, Linda, and Glenna Gerard. *Dialogue: Rediscover the Transforming Power of Conversation*. New York: Wiley, 1998.

Isaacs, William. *Dialogue: The Art of Thinking Together*. New York: Doubleday,1999.

Stone, Douglas, Bruce Patton, and Sheila Heen. *Difficult Conversations: How to Discuss What Matters Most*. New York: Penguin, 2010.

Wheatley, Margaret. *Turning to One Another: Simple Conversations to Restore Hope to the Future*. San Francisco: Berrett-Koehler, 2009.

Formation and Spiritual Direction

Barry, William A. *Finding God in All Things: A Companion to the Spiritual Exercises of St. Ignatius*. Notre Dame, IN: Ave Maria Press, 1991.

Barry, William A., and William J. Connolly. *The Practice of Spiritual Direction* (2nd ed. rev.). San Francisco: HarperCollins, 1982.

Bellah, Robert N. *Religion in Human Evolution: From the Paleolithic to the Axial Age*. Cambridge, MA: Belknap Press of Harvard University Press, 2011.

Bellah, Robert N., Richard Madsen, William M. Sullivan, Ann Swidler, and Steven M. Tipton. *Habits of the Heart: Individualism and Commitment in American Life*. Berkeley, CA: University of California Press, 1996.

Benner, David G. *Sacred Companions: The Gift of Spiritual Friendship and Direction*. Downers Grove, IL: Intervarsity Press, 2002.

Fernandez-Carvajal, Frances. *Through Wind and Waves: On Being a Spiritual Guide*. New York: Scepter Publishers, 2012.

Frankl, Viktor. *Man's Search for Meaning*. Boston: Beacon Press, 2006.

Lawrence-Lightfoot, Sarah. *Respect: An Exploration*. New York: Basic Books, 2000.

Lewis, C. S. *The Abolition of Man.* New York: HarperCollins, 2001.

Maslow, A. H. *The Farther Reaches of Human Nature.* New York: Penguin, 1993.

Maslow, A. H. *Toward a Psychology of Being.* Blacksburg, VA: Wilder Publications, 2011.

Merton, Thomas. *Spiritual Direction and Meditation.* Collegeville, MN: Order of St. Benedict, 1960.

Nepo, Mark. *The Book of Awakening: Having the Life You Want by Being Present to the Life You Have.* San Francisco: Conari Press, 2011.

Nouwen, Henri. *Spiritual Formation: Following the Movements of the Spirit.* New York: HarperCollins, 2010.

Palmer, Parker J. "Divided No More: A Movement Approach to Educational Reform." *Change* 24, no. 2 (March–April 1992): 10–17.

Palmer, Parker J. *A Hidden Wholeness: The Journey Toward an Undivided Life.* San Francisco: Jossey-Bass, 2004.

Rabow, M. W., C. Evans, and R. N. Remen. "Professional Deformation: Student's Perceptions of Repression of Personal Values and Qualities in Medical Education." *Teaching and Learning in MedicineTeaching and Learning in Medicine* 24 (2012): 91.

Rabow, M. W., C. Evans, and R. N. Remen. "Professional Formation and Deformation: Repression of Personal Values and Qualities in Medical Education." *Family Medicine* (forthcoming).

Rabow, M. W., R. N. Remen, D. X. Parmelee, and T. S. Inui. "Professional Formation: Extending Medicine's Lineage of Service into the Next Century." *Academic MedicineAcademic Medicine* 85 (2010): 310–317.

St. Ignatius of Loyola. *Spiritual Exercises of St. Ignatius*. Trans. Anthony Mattola. New York: Doubleday Dell, 1989.

Zajonc, Arthur. *Meditation as Contemplative Inquiry*. Great Barrington, MA: SteinerBooks/Anthroposophic Press, 2009.

Mentoring

Bland, Carole J., Anne L. Taylor, Lynn S. Shollen, Anne Marie Weber-Main, and Patricia A. Mulcahy. *Faculty Success Through Mentoring: A Guide for Mentors, Mentees, and Leaders*. Lanham, MD: Rowan & Littlefield, 2009.

Huang, Chungliang A. *Mentoring: The Tao of Giving and Receiving Wisdom*. San Francisco: HarperCollins, 1995.

Huang, Chungliang A., and Jerry Lynch. *Tao Mentoring: Cultivating Collaborative Relationships in All Areas of Your Life*. New York: Marlowe and Company, 1995.

Johnson, W. Brad. *On Being a Mentor: A Guide for Higher Education Faculty*. Mahwah, NJ: Erlbaum, 2006.

Maxwell, John. *Mentoring 101: What Every Leader Needs to Know*. Nashville, TN: Thomas Nelson, 2008.

Nakamura, Jeanne, and David J. Shernoff. *Good Mentoring: Fostering Excellent Practice in Higher Education*. San Francisco: Jossey-Bass, 2009.

Parks, Sharon. *Big Questions, Worthy Dreams: Mentoring Emerging Adults in Their Search for Meaning, Purpose, and Faith*. San Francisco: Jossey-Bass, 2010.

UMASS Amherst. *Mutual Mentoring Guide*. 2009. http://www.umass.edu/ctfd/mentoring/downloads/Mutual%20Mentoring%20Guide%20Final%2011_20.pdf.2009.

Zachary, Lois J. *The Mentee's Guide: Making Mentoring Work for You*. San Francisco: Jossey-Bass, 2009.

Zachary, Lois J. *The Mentor's Guide: Facilitating Effective Learning Relationships* (2nd ed.). San Francisco: Jossey-Bass, 2011.

Community

Block, Peter. *Community: The Structure of Belonging*. San Francisco: Berrett-Koehler, 2008.

Gladwell, M. *The Tipping Point: How Little Things Can Make a Big Difference* (2nd ed.). New York: Little, Brown, 2000.

Healing the Heart of Diversity. 2000. http://www.newdimensions .org/program-archive/healing-the-heart-of-diversity-with-pat-harbour-paul-schultz-shirley-strong-jimmy-carter-martina-whelsula-sally-huang-nissen-roosevelt-thomas-louis-ervin-amshatar-monroe

Kegan, Robert. *Immunity to Change: How to Overcome It and Unlock the Potential in Yourself and Your Organization*. Boston: Harvard Business School Publishing, 2009.

McKnight, John, and Peter Block. *The Abundant Community: Awakening the Power of Families and Neighborhoods*. San Francisco: Berrett-Koehler, 2012.

Putnam, Robert D. *Bowling Alone: The Collapse and Revival of American Community*. New York: Simon and Schuster, 2000.

Putnam, Robert D., Lewis Feldstein, and Donald J. Cohen. *Better Together: Restoring the American Community*. New York: Simon and Schuster, 2003.

Rabow, M., J. Wrubel, and R. Remen. "Authentic Community as an Educational Strategy in Professionalism: A National Evaluation of the Healer's Art Curriculum." *Journal of General and Internal Medicine* 221 (2007): 1422–1428.

Wheatley, Margaret, and Deborah Frieze. *Walk Out Walk On: A Learning Journey into Communities Daring to Live the Future Now*. San Francisco: Berrett-Koehler, 2011.

Wheatley, Margaret, and Myron Kellner-Roger. *A Simpler Way*. San Francisco: Berrett-Koehler, 1996.

Websites

We recommend going to the websites of Rachel Naomi Remen's organizations: ISHI: Institute for the Study of Health and Illness, http://www.ishiprograms.org/; Remembering the Heart of Medicine, http://theheartofmedicine.org/; Commonweal, http://www.commonweal.org/.

O'Neill, Patrick. *Extraordinary Conversations*. Toronto, Canada. http://www.extraordinaryconversations.com

NOTES

Introduction

1. The project was led by Mark Nepo, Sharon Daloz Parks, and Arthur Zajonc, who invited a cadre of distinguished mentors, including Angeles Arrien, Alexander and Helen Astin, Rita Charon, Manuel Gomez, Robert McDermott, Parker J.Palmer, Peter Schneider, Rachel Naomi Remen, Paul Wapner, Diana Chapman Walsh, and Eileen Wilson-Oyelaran.

2. Rachel Naomi Remen, *Finding Meaning in Medicine Resource Guide* (Bolinas, CA: Institute for the Study of Health and Illness Press, 2002). Angeles Arrien, *The Four-Fold Way: Walking the Paths of the Warrior, Teacher, Healer and Visionary* (San Francisco: HarperCollins, 1993).

Chapter One: What Is a Formation Mentoring Community?

1. Robert D. Putnam, *Bowling Alone: The Collapse and Revival of American Community* (New York: Simon & Shuster, 2001).

2. Parker J. Palmer and Arthur Zajonc, *The Heart of Higher Education: A Call to Renewal* (San Francisco: Jossey-Bass, 2010), 13.

3. Martin Seligman, *Authentic Happiness: Using the New Positive Psychology to Realize Your Potential for Lasting Fulfillment*

(New York: Simon & Schuster, 2004). Christopher Peterson, *A Primer in Positive Psychology* (New York: Oxford University Press, 2006).

4. Alasdair MacIntyre, *After Virtue*, 3rd ed. (Notre Dame, IN: University of Notre Dame Press, 1984).

5. Lois J. Zachary, *The Mentor's Guide: Facilitating Effective Learning Relationships* (San Francisco: Jossey-Bass, 2011); Lois J. Zachary and Lory A. Fischler, *The Mentee's Guide: Making Mentoring Work for You* (San Francisco: Jossey-Bass, 2009); and Lois J. Zachary, *Creating a Mentoring Culture: The Organization's Guide* (San Francisco: Jossey-Bass, 2005).

6. Carole J. Bland, Anne L. Taylor, Lynn S. Shollen, Anne Marie Weber-Main, and Patricia A. Mulcahy, *Faculty Success Through Mentoring: A Guide for Mentors, Mentees, and Leaders* (Lanham, MD: Rowan & Littlefield, 2009). W. Brad Johnson, *On Being a Mentor: A Guide for Higher Education Faculty* (Mahwah, NJ: Erlbaum, 2006), ix.

7. Sharon Parks, *Big Questions, Worthy Dreams: Mentoring Emerging Adults in Their Search for Meaning, Purpose, and Faith* (San Francisco: Jossey-Bass, 2010).

8. David Bohm, *On Dialogue* (New York: Routledge, 1996).

9. Peter Block, *Community: The Structure of Belonging* (San Francisco: Berrett-Koehler, 2008). Sara Lawrence-Lightfoot, *Respect: An Exploration* (New York: Basic Books, 2000). Craig Neal and Patricia Neal, *The Art of Convening: Authentic Engagement in Meetings, Gatherings, and Conversations* (San Francisco: Berrett-Koehler, 2011).

10. For more on Aristotle's concepts of friendship and its relationship to FMCs, see chapter 2.

Interlude: Message in a Bottle

1. Walker Percy, *Signposts in a Strange Land* (New York: Farrar, Strauss & Giroux, 1991). Some readers might be familiar with "Message in a Bottle" (The Police, Regatta de Blanc, 1979), a song inspired by Walker Percy's essay.
2. Percy, *Signposts in a Strange Land*, 359.
3. Ibid.

Chapter Two: Cultivating Growth

1. Parker J. Palmer, *To Know as We Are Known: Education as a Spiritual Journey* (San Francisco: HarperSanFrancisco, 1993), 74.
2. Ibid.
3. Parker J. Palmer, *The Courage to Teach* (San Francisco: Jossey-Bass, 1998), 73–77.
4. Constantin Brancusi, quoted in D. Bayles and T. Orland, *Art and Fear: Observations on the Perils (and Rewards) of Artmaking* (Santa Cruz, CA: Image Continuum, 1993), 65.
5. A. L. Antonio, M. J. Chang, K. Hakuta, D. A. Kenny, S. L. Levin, and J. F. Milem, "Effects of Racial Diversity on Complex Thinking in College Students," *Psychological Science* 15 (2004): 507–510.
6. David Bohm, *On Dialogue* (New York: Routledge, 1996).
7. Rainer Maria Rilke, *Letters to a Young Poet*, translated by M. D. Hert Norton (New York: Norton, 1934), p. 35.
8. Miller McPherson, Lynn Smith-Lovin, and Matthew E. Brashears, "Social Isolation in America: Changes in Core

Discussion Networks over Two Decades," *American Sociological Review* 71 (2006): 353–375.

9. Robert D. Putnam, *Bowling Alone: The Collapse and Revival of American Community* (New York: Simon & Shuster, 2001).

Chapter Three: The Basics of Creating Formation Mentoring Communities on Your Campus

1. "Why Academics Suffer Burnout," *Chronicle of Higher Education*, April 14, 2011, http://www.insidehighered.com/news /2011/04/14/research_analyzes_burnout_of_faculty_members _all_over_the_world.
2. For more information on Finding Meaning in Medicine, see http://www.ishiprograms.org/programs/all-healthcare-professionals/.
3. Rachel Naomi Remen, *Finding Meaning in Medicine Resource Guide* (Bolinas, CA: Institute for the Study of Health and Illness Press, 2002), http://www.ishiprograms.org/findingmeaning.
4. Peter Block, *Community: The Structure of Belonging* (San Francisco: Berrett-Koehler, 2008).
5. Angeles Arrien, *The Four-Fold Way: Walking the Paths of the Warrior, Teacher, Healer and Visionary* (San Francisco: HarperCollins, 1993), 7–8.
6. Remen, *Finding Meaning in Medicine Resource Guide.*
7. Ibid.
8. Adapted from Rachel Naomi Remen, "The Healer's Art Resource Guide."

Chapter Four: Collaborative Stewardship

1. Rachel Naomi Remen, *Finding Meaning in Medicine Resource Guide* (Bolinas, CA: Institute for the Study of Health and Illness Press, 2002), http://www.ishiprograms.org/finding meaning.

2. A copy of "Seasons" can be downloaded at http://www.fetzer .org/sites/default/files/images/stories/pdf/seasonsbook.pdf.

3. Angeles Arrien, *Living in Gratitude: A Journey That Will Change Your Life* (Louisville, CO: Sounds True Publishing, 2010).

4. Angeles Arrien, *The Second Half of Life* (Louisville, CO: Sounds True Publishing, 2005).

5. Naomi Shihab Nye, "How Things Could Be," March 5, 2010, http://www.gratefulness.org/readings/nye_gate.htm.

Chapter Five: From Individual to Institutional Change

1. Richard L. Morrill, *Strategic Leadership: Integrating Strategy and Leadership in Colleges and Universities* (Lanham, MD: Rowan & Littlefield, 2010).

2. Clayton M. Christensen and Henry J. Eyring, *The Innovative University: Changing the DNA of Higher Education from the Inside Out* (San Francisco: Jossey-Bass, 2011).

3. Parker J. Palmer, "Divided No More: A Movement Approach to Educational Reform," *Change Magazine* 24 (March–April 1992): 12.

4. Ibid.

5. For more information, on the Courage to Teach and Lead movement, go to the Center for Courage and Renewal website: http://www.couragerenewal.org/.

Afterword

1. Rachel Naomi Remen, *Finding Meaning in Medicine Resource Guide* (Bolinas, CA: Institute for the Study of Health and Illness Press, 2002), http://www.ishiprograms.org/findingmeaning.

2. Mark Nepo, *The Book of Awakening: Having the Life You Want by Being Present to the Life You Have* (San Francisco: Conari Press, 2011).

GRATITUDES

The most important things are always the hardest to say. As we mentioned in chapter 1, this book belongs as much to Angeles Arrien and Rachel Naomi Remen as it does to the four authors. To call Angeles and Rachel simply "mentors"—and they certainly were that—would be to diminish the role they have played in this work and in our lives. The four of us consider them to be among the most extraordinary individuals we have known. They gave us not only their advice and wisdom, but truly gave of themselves. To have spent so much time in their company has been a tremendous privilege.

This book was written by a group of authors who never would have begun, much less completed, it without the support of a much larger group of mentors and collaborators. To edit a "single voice" book written by four authors requires an editor who is both remarkably daring and skilled. Megan Scribner managed to shape our disparate pieces into a coherent whole with an understanding of us and our dream of higher education that was both intuitive and astonishing and with a patience that was awesome.

Our editor at Jossey-Bass, Sheryl Fullerton, had the vision to see what formation mentoring communities (FMCs) could do in higher education and took a chance on this unusual book. We thank Sheryl for her work in shepherding the book to completion.

Mark Nepo, who led the initial gatherings sponsored by the Fetzer Institute, showed us by example how to convene a group of individuals who had just met in a way that quickly brings the group to a place of depth and substance. Sharon Daloz Parks and Arthur Zajonc continued to lead this larger group with skill and grace, and they encouraged our small group in our work with FMCs and in the writing of this book.

This project would not have gotten under way or continued without the financial support provided by the Fetzer Institute. We extend our gratitude also to Eileen Wilson-Oyelaran and Kalamazoo College for their continued administrative support when the project changed hands. During our larger gatherings, we were privileged to be mentored by Parker J. Palmer, Diana Chapman Walsh, and Helen and Alexander Astin—the project's "visiting elders" who gave generously of their time and their wisdom.

Tenzin Lhadron and Heidi Ihrig, who made sure that our gatherings ran smoothly, were always helpful and unfailingly warm and hospitable. Jennifer Walls and Allison Shrier helped coordinate our weekly phone calls, which kept us talking and writing between meetings, and Allison provided technical support with using newfangled online writing tools that proved quite useful.

The Intergenerational Mentoring Project involved a truly extraordinary group of colleagues whom we are now honored to call friends. All of them in some way or another helped to shape this book. We thank the senior mentors in this group. In addition to Angeles and Rachel, they included Rita Charon, Manuel Gomez, Robert McDermott, Peter Schneider, Paul Wapner, and Eileen Wilson-Oyelaran. Finally, we thank the junior members of this project: Anthony Antonio, Rebecca Gould, Nawang Phuntsog, Matthew Jelacic, Ann Jurecic, Kat Vlahos, Bruce Miller, Regina Stevens-Truss, Victoria Maizes, and Cyd Jenefsky.

We also have some individual thanks to give:

Dirksen: I thank my wife, Nicole Salimbene, for her contributions to the ideas and questions throughout chapter 2. Without calling it such, she has been engaged in formation work throughout her life. Her wisdom and insights have always been deeply instructive for me, and now they can be for readers as well. I also thank the members of my FMC—Robert Sirvage, Melissa Malzkuhn, and Michelle McAuliffe—for their partnership in our transformative work. I am honored to be in their company.

Aaron: I thank my wife, Jennifer, who put up with my late-night writing and the many trips to Sausalito and Kalamazoo. I also thank all the members of my FMC: Rebecca Hedrick, Gail Ryan-Raphael, Toni Lynn Pusateri, Atur Turakhia, Larry Faziola, and Matthew Butteri. They have inspired me and given me hope for the future of medical education.

Peter: I am grateful for the love and encouragement of Sara, Katie, and Timothy. You inspire me every day. I also thank Samantha DiRosa, Mary Knight-McKenna, Darris Means, and Nina Namaste for creating and nurturing the Elon FMC with me. Our conversations give me purpose and hope. I can't wait for the next one.

Ed: I am grateful to be at a university that is capable of remarkable acts of caring, decency, and compassion. I thank the members of my mentoring group. My dear friends Arthur and Larry have been a source of eternal love, hope, and compassion. Bennett and Evan: I love you and dedicate my work to you.

ABOUT THE AUTHORS

Angeles Arrien is a cultural anthropologist, author, educator, and consultant to many organizations and businesses. She lectures and conducts workshops worldwide, bridging cultural anthropology, psychology, and comparative religions. For over thirty-five years, Arrien has included within her Four-Fold Way educational programs three-day solo wilderness experiences in northern California and Arizona. The heart of her work supports thousands of people nationally and internationally, from the ages of sixteen to eighty-seven, to reconnect to nature and to themselves.

She is the founder and president of the Foundation for Cross-Cultural Education and Research, and the author of seven books. Among them are *The Four-Fold Way; Signs of Life* (winner of the 1993 Benjamin Franklin Award), and *The Second Half of Life* (winner of the 2007 Nautilus Award for Best Book on Aging). Her latest book, *Living in Gratitude: A Journey That Will Change Your Life*, was the Gold Medal cowinner of the 2012 Independent Publisher Book Awards in the category of inspiration/spirituality. Her books have been translated into thirteen languages, and she has received three honorary doctorate degrees in recognition of her work.

❧

H-Dirksen L. Bauman is professor of Deaf Studies at Gallaudet University, where he serves as department chair, coordinator for the master's program in Deaf Studies, and coordinator for the Office of Bilingual Teaching and Learning. He is the coeditor of the book/DVD project, *Signing the Body Poetic: Essays in American Sign Language* (2006) and editor of *Open Your Eyes: Deaf Studies Talking* (2008). Dirksen is also a producer and codirector of the film *Audism Unveiled* (2008) and producer of the film *Gallaudet*. He currently serves as co–executive editor of *Deaf Studies Digital Journal*, the world's first peer-reviewed academic and cultural arts journal to feature scholarship and creative work in both signed and written languages.

Dirksen received his B.A. in English from Colorado College and then worked as a dormitory supervisor at the Colorado School for the Deaf and the Blind, where he acquired his new-found identity as a hearing person. At that school, he became interested in the study of sign language literature. He then pursued an M.A. degree in English from the University of Northern Colorado and a Ph.D. in English from Binghamton University, State University of New York. He has held teaching positions at the National Technical Institute for the Deaf at the Rochester Institute of Technology and in the Department of English at Gallaudet University. He has published articles on American Sign Language literature, autobiographical practices, audism, bioethics, and Deaf Gain, the notion that reverses the concept of hearing loss to explore the cognitive, creative, and cultural assets that have arisen from Deaf communities.

❧

Peter Felten is assistant provost for teaching and learning, director of the Center for Engaged Learning, executive director of the Center for the Advancement of Teaching and Learning, and associate professor of history at Elon University. He has published and presented widely on engaged learning, faculty development, and the scholarship of teaching and learning. His recent research explores the possibilities of student-faculty partnerships in teaching and learning. He has served as president of the POD Network, an international association for teaching and learning centers in higher education. He also has been a fellow of the Andrew W. Mellon Teaching and Learning Institute at Bryn Mawr College.

He is a graduate of Marquette University, and earned his Ph.D. in history from the University of Texas at Austin.

❧

Aaron Kheriaty is the director of residency training and medical education in the Department of Psychiatry at the University of California, Irvine (UCI). He also serves as codirector of the Program in Medical Ethics at the UCI School of Medicine and chairs the clinical ethics committee at UCI Medical Center.

He graduated from the University of Notre Dame in philosophy and premedical sciences and earned his medical degree from Georgetown University School of Medicine. He has published and lectured internationally to professional and lay audiences on topics related to medical education, psychiatry, ethics, religion, and spirituality.

Kheriaty founded and directed the Psychiatry and Spirituality Forum at UCI, a five-year interdisciplinary project (2006–2010). The forum was dedicated to recognizing, appreciating, and exploring the connection between patients' mental health and their spiritual, religious, philosophical, and moral convictions. His recent book, *The Catholic Guide to Depression* (2012), developed out of the forum's work.

In addition to teaching and supervision of medical students and psychiatry residents, Kheriaty maintains a part-time outpatient practice in general adult psychiatry. He serves on the board of directors for J Serra Catholic High School.

~<><>~

Rachel Naomi Remen is clinical professor of family and community medicine at the University of California, San Francisco, School of Medicine, where she developed the Healer's Art, a curriculum in formation for medical students taught annually by faculty in more than half of American medical schools and schools in seven other countries. She is a pioneer in the field of integrative medicine and relationship-centered care and relationship-centered medical education and is the author of one of the earliest books on whole person medicine, *The Human Patient* (1981). She is the founder and director of the Institute for the Study of Health and Illness at Commonweal, a professional development institute. Through her national postgraduate continuing education initiatives, thousands of physicians, nurses, and other health professionals have studied and practiced the principles and practices of a medicine of healing.

Remen is a graduate of Weill Cornell Medical College and Stanford University School of Medicine and holds four honorary degrees. She has lectured and published extensively on formation in professional education, and her award-winning books, *Kitchen Table Wisdom* and *My Grandfather's Blessings*, have been translated into twenty-two languages.

~<><>~

Ed Taylor is vice provost and dean of undergraduate academic affairs at the University of Washington: Seattle, where he oversees educational opportunities that deepen and enrich the undergraduate experience, including first-year programs, the Office of Educational Assessment, experiential learning, academic advising and support, and the university honors program.

He joined the UW's College of Education in 1995 as an assistant professor. His research and teaching center on the historical and moral dimensions of education, education and social justice, and leadership. He has taught, presented, and written extensively on these topics.

Taylor earned his Ph.D. in educational leadership and policy studies from the University of Washington. At Gonzaga University, he earned a master's degree in psychology and bachelor's degrees in sociology and psychology.

Active in the community, Taylor is a trustee at Gonzaga University and a founding board member of Rainier Scholars.

INDEX